Translanguaging in Multicultural Societies

Lucila María Pérez Fernández

Translanguaging in Multicultural Societies

Beyond Borders

Lucila María Pérez Fernández
University of Cantabria
Santander, Spain

ISBN 978-3-031-74144-9   ISBN 978-3-031-74145-6 (eBook)
https://doi.org/10.1007/978-3-031-74145-6

Cover credit: © Melisa Hasan

This Palgrave Macmillan imprint is published by the registered company Springer Nature Switzerland AG
The registered company address is: Gewerbestrasse 11, 6330 Cham, Switzerland

If disposing of this product, please recycle the paper.

CONTENTS

CHAPTER 1

Introduction

Abstract This chapter serves as an introduction to the concept of translanguaging, tracing its origins and exploring its evolution from a pedagogical strategy in bilingual education to a broader framework that challenges traditional language boundaries. It examines how translanguaging has grown to influence various domains and distinguishes it from related practices such as code-switching, emphasizing its significance in diverse linguistic environments. This chapter concludes by outlining the structure of the book.

Keywords Translanguaging · Multilingualism · Code-switching · Language education · Linguistic diversity

The term "translanguaging" traces its origins to the Welsh term "trawsieithu," a concept initially coined by Cen Williams (1996) and later translated into English by Baker (2001). This concept was introduced as a pedagogical strategy to encourage bilingual students to draw on both their languages to enhance learning. Initially, it denoted a pedagogical practice involving the intentional use of two languages in educational settings. However, as we traverse the twenty-first century, the concept of translanguaging has evolved into a broader framework that encompasses linguistic, cognitive, and social processes. The work of scholars like García

© The Author(s), under exclusive license to Springer Nature
Switzerland AG 2024
L. M. Pérez Fernández, *Translanguaging in Multicultural Societies*,
https://doi.org/10.1007/978-3-031-74145-6_1

1

and Li (2014) has expanded our understanding of translanguaging as a phenomenon that transcends linguistic boundaries, challenging traditional notions of language separation and purity.

At its core, translanguaging involves the fluid use of multiple languages to create meaning, breaking away from rigid monolingual ideologies. This multidimensional practice is not confined to classrooms; it unfolds in a variety of social environments where people interact using the full range of their linguistic capabilities. Translanguaging recognizes that language is not a fixed entity but a flexible resource that evolves depending on context, purpose, and audience.

In bilingual and multilingual environments, speakers often engage in translanguaging as a natural response to their linguistic needs. Li (2000) highlights that bilingual individuals regularly switch between languages, not just out of necessity but also to reflect cultural identities and social relationships. This fluid movement between languages, whether spoken or written, is not merely incidental but forms a central aspect of how bilinguals manage communication in diverse settings. One form of this language alternation is code-switching, which involves switching between languages within or between sentences. However, code-switching and translanguaging are distinct practices. Code-switching has often been viewed negatively, as a disruption to communication rather than a valuable linguistic resource (Grosjean, 1989). For example, it is sometimes seen as a result of inadequate L2 knowledge (Nnenna et al., 2022), such as a lack of vocabulary or grammar, or as an avoidance strategy, where speakers switch to their first language (L1) to bypass the difficulty of using the L2. In contrast, translanguaging is a more intentional and holistic practice, involving the strategic use of an individual's entire linguistic repertoire in various modes, including spoken, written, and visual forms, to enhance communication and learning (García & Li, 2014).

The transformative nature of translanguaging is particularly evident when examined through multiple perspectives. From a sociolinguistic viewpoint, it challenges traditional notions of language boundaries and hierarchies, highlighting how multilingual practices shape and reflect social identities and power dynamics. Psycholinguistically, it offers insights into cognitive processes involved in managing and integrating multiple languages, shedding light on the mental mechanisms underpinning language use. Sociopolitically, translanguaging serves as a tool for resistance and empowerment within marginalized communities. It provides a means for asserting cultural identity and challenging monolingual norms imposed by dominant linguistic frameworks.

Pedagogically, translanguaging extends beyond mere instructional strategies to encompass broader educational philosophies that value and harness linguistic diversity. The educational sphere has witnessed a profound impact partly due to globalization. The foreign language classroom, once a homogeneous space, has transformed into a superdiverse environment (Blommaert & Rampton, 2011). This diversity reflected in student demographics presents new challenges to traditional norms established in the monolingual era. Learners with multilingual backgrounds are becoming more prevalent due to factors like immigration, the promotion of early language learning, and the internationalization of higher education. Amid the shifting paradigms in language education, translanguaging emerges as a transformative educational strategy in language teaching, a domain where the monolingual principle has been unwittingly implemented and reinforced by numerous teachers (Wang & Curdt-Christiansen, 2019). Its potential advantages, as elucidated by Baker (2001), extend beyond conventional language acquisition by enhancing subject understanding and bolstering weaker languages. It facilitates home–school links, cooperation, and the integration of fluent speakers with early learners. Furthermore, the cognitive processing involved in translanguaging, as emphasized by Baker (2001), contributes to the retention and development of bilingualism. Additionally, multilinguals, equipped with broader repertoires, bring valuable experiences to the language learning process (Cenoz & Gorter, 2021).

Nevertheless, in contemporary discussions, translanguaging is no longer confined to the classroom; it now encompasses a wide array of linguistic practices that occur in diverse environments, from professional settings to digital spaces. Professionals across various sectors, from business to healthcare, are finding that translanguaging allows them to engage more effectively with clients, colleagues, and communities who speak different languages. As noted by Sato (2023), translanguaging in these contexts is often a natural, intuitive process that reflects the speaker's need to convey meaning as effectively as possible. This broader understanding challenges traditional language boundaries and reflects a more holistic view of bilingualism and multilingualism. Grosjean (1982) criticized the expectation that bilingual individuals should function as two monolinguals in one, highlighting the artificiality of such a demand. Instead, translanguaging practices reflect the reality that bilinguals draw on their entire linguistic repertoire in ways that cannot be easily compartmentalized into distinct languages.

Moreover, translanguaging has been recognized as a powerful force in social and political movements, particularly for language-minoritized communities enabling individuals to break free from the historical constraints imposed by language hierarchies and serving as a mirror that authentically reflects their linguistic identities. By embracing translanguaging, communities can challenge dominant monolingual norms and advocate for more inclusive practices that recognize and celebrate the richness of multilingual communication (Cenoz & Gorter, 2022). This has important implications for fields such as social justice, where language plays a crucial role in the struggle for equity and representation.

In summary, translanguaging has grown from a pedagogical concept to a multifaceted phenomenon with broad implications across numerous fields. It challenges traditional views of language as a series of separate, monolithic systems and instead positions language as a fluid, dynamic resource that individuals draw upon to navigate a complex world.

This book explores how translanguaging functions across diverse domains, examining its potential as a powerful tool for communication, learning, and identity construction. The narrative is structured across four distinct parts, each carefully crafted to unravel the layers of translanguaging's influence across different spheres.

Part I: Understanding Translanguaging (Chapters 2–4) lays the groundwork, introducing the concept of translanguaging and exploring the core principles of translanguaging theory, thereby establishing a solid theoretical foundation. After this, the section explores the historical evolution of multilingual practices, tracing their roots from early multilingual societies through colonial and postcolonial contexts to the present globalized world. Additionally, it examines the impact of various language policies on translanguaging, contrasting government-led frameworks with non-government approaches.

Part II: Theoretical Foundations (Chapters 5–8) guides the reader through the theoretical underpinnings of translanguaging by drawing from diverse fields such as sociolinguistics, cognitive science, and psycholinguistics. It discusses how sociolinguistic theories address language variation and multilingualism, emphasizing the relationship between language, culture, and social identity, and examines cognitive approaches to translanguaging, highlighting connections with metacognitive processes and cognitive flexibility. The section also presents psycholinguistic perspectives, focusing on the psychological and emotional aspects of translanguaging, and aligns these insights with broader sociocultural theories to demonstrate how translanguaging supports cultural practices and knowledge.

Part III: Translanguaging in Practice (Chapters 9–11) bridges theory and application, exploring its role in various real-world settings. This section explores how translanguaging can be effectively integrated into multilingual classrooms by providing strategies and best practices for language teaching, and discussing the benefits and challenges educators may encounter. It also examines the role of translanguaging in multicultural communities, highlighting its importance in community development, social integration, and cultural heritage preservation. Additionally, the section considers the use of translanguaging in professional environments, including the business sector, healthcare settings, and legal and ethical contexts, demonstrating its wide-ranging impact and applicability.

Part IV: Future Directions (Chapters 12–14) looks ahead to the evolving field of translanguaging, particularly in relation to emerging technologies and global initiatives. It explores the potential of translanguaging in virtual reality and augmented reality applications, as well as its integration with artificial intelligence and machine learning. The section also addresses the role of translanguaging in the preservation and revitalization of indigenous and minority languages, emphasizing its importance in maintaining linguistic diversity. Finally, it connects translanguaging to the United Nations' Sustainable Development Goals, illustrating how multilingual education and linguistic diversity can contribute to achieving quality education and reducing inequalities on a global scale. This section sets the stage for future research, envisioning the continued evolution and application of translanguaging principles.

The book culminates with Chapter 15, Conclusion, where we synthesize the key insights gathered from the preceding chapters and propose avenues for future research.

REFERENCES

Baker, C. (2001, 2011). *Foundations of bilingual education and bilingualism.* Multilingual Matters.
Blommaert, J., & Rampton, B. (2011). *Language and Superdiversity. Diversities,* *13*(2), 1–21.

Cenoz, J., & Gorter, D. (2021). *Pedagogical Translanguaging*. Cambridge University Press.

Cenoz, J., & Gorter, D. (2022). Pedagogical translanguaging and its application to language classes. *RELC Journal, 53*(2), 342–354. https://doi.org/10.1177/00336882221082751

García, O., & Li, W. (2014). *Translanguaging: Language, bilingualism and education*. Palgrave Macmillan.

Grosjean, F. (1982). *Life with two languages*. Harvard University Press.

Grosjean, F. (1989). Neurolinguists, beware! The bilingual is not two monolinguals in one person. *Brain and Language, 36*(1), 3–15. https://doi.org/10.1016/0093-934x(89)90048-5

Li, W. (2000). Dimensions of bilingualism. In W. Li (Ed.), *The bilingualism reader* (pp. 3–25). Routledge.

Li, W., & García, O. (2022). Not a first language but one repertoire: Translanguaging as a decolonizing project. *RELC Journal, 53*(2), 313–324. https://doi.org/10.1177/00336882221092841

Nnenna, E., & I., A., O., Umeh, E., Chikaodi, A. (2022). Code switching and code mixing in teaching and learning of English as a second language: Building on knowledge. *English Language Teaching, 15*(9), 106–106. https://doi.org/10.5539/elt.v15n9p106

Sato, R. (2023). Japanese EFL Speakers' willingness to communicate in L2 conversations: The Effects of code-switching and translanguaging. *The Electronic Journal for English as a Second Language, 27*(3), 1–22. https://doi.org/10.55593/ej.27107a5

Wang, W., & Curdt-Christiansen, X. L. (2019). Translanguaging in a Chinese-English bilingual education programme: A university-classroom ethnography. *International Journal of Bilingual Education and Bilingualism, 22*(3), 322–337. https://doi.org/10.1080/13670050.2018.1526254

Williams, C. (1996). Secondary education: Teaching in the bilingual situation. In C. Williams, G. Lewis, & C. Baker (Eds.), *The language policy: Taking stock* (pp. 39–78). CAI Language Studies Centre.

PART I

Understanding Translanguaging

CHAPTER 2

Defining Translanguaging

Abstract This chapter delves into the concept of translanguaging, tracing its development from a tool in language education to a broader approach to multilingual communication. It contrasts translanguaging with code-switching, emphasizing their distinct characteristics and underlying principles. The chapter also explores core premises of translanguaging theory, highlighting its flexibility in language practices, alignment with multicompetence, and role in challenging language hierarchies.

Keywords Translanguaging · Multilingual communication · Code-switching · Language education · Multicompetence · Language practices · Language hierarchies

Translanguaging, a term rooted in language education, has evolved into a comprehensive concept that transcends mere language instruction. García (2009b) defines translanguaging as "the act performed by bilinguals of accessing different linguistic features or various modes of what are described as autonomous languages, in order to maximize communicative potential" (p. 140). Central to understanding translanguaging is the idea that it involves more than just the use of multiple languages; it represents a holistic approach where linguistic resources are drawn upon seamlessly to communicate effectively.

© The Author(s), under exclusive license to Springer Nature Switzerland AG 2024
L. M. Pérez Fernández, *Translanguaging in Multicultural Societies*,
https://doi.org/10.1007/978-3-031-74145-6_2

Initially introduced by Cen Williams in the context of Welsh bilingual education, translanguaging originally described a pedagogical practice where input (e.g., reading and/or listening) occurred in one language, while output (e.g., speaking and/or writing) took place in another (Williams, 1996). This approach was innovative at the time because it directly challenged the prevailing monolingual ethos in the Welsh educational system, where bilingual talk was often viewed as problematic rather than as a valuable resource (Lewis et al., 2012b). Translanguaging emerged as a strategic practice, designed to leverage the full linguistic repertoire of bilingual students, allowing them to shift between languages fluidly to reinforce both languages and enhance understanding. As Williams (1996) described, "translanguaging means that you receive information through the medium of one language (e.g., English) and use it through the medium of the other language (e.g., Welsh)" (p. 64). Baker (2011) further explored translanguaging's potential in developing academic language skills in both languages arguing for its relevance in all bilingual educational contexts, not just within Wales. He emphasized that translanguaging is about making meaning in two languages and can be employed in a planned, developmental, and strategic manner to maximize students' linguistic and cognitive capabilities while reflecting the sociocultural nature of language.

As translanguaging expanded beyond the classroom, it began to encompass the spontaneous and conscious use of multiple languages in everyday life reflecting how bilingual and multilingual speakers naturally draw on their entire linguistic repertoire to communicate more effectively in diverse social contexts (Cenoz & Gorter, 2017; Creese & Blackledge, 2010; Li, 2018). García (2009a) broadened the definition of translanguaging to include "multiple discursive practices in which bilinguals engage in order to make sense of their bilingual worlds" (p. 45). This shift moves beyond the educational realm, illusrating how translanguaging occurs in various domains of life, including informal and social interactions. Supporting this broader application, Lewis et al. (2012a) noted that the concept of translanguaging "has been generalized from school to street, from pedagogical practices to everyday cognitive processing, from classroom lessons to all contexts of a bilingual's life" (p. 647). This evolution underscores the idea that translanguaging is not just an educational tool but a natural aspect of bilingual and multilingual individuals' daily lives.

One significant insight from translanguaging scholarship is that it challenges the traditional view of languages as discrete, bounded systems. Instead, it posits that multilingual speakers fluidly use their linguistic resources without compartmentalizing them into separate languages. As noted by Otheguy et al. (2015), this perspective highlights the socially constructed nature of "named languages" (specific languages that societies formally recognize and label, such as English and Spanish) and the artificial boundaries imposed by sociopolitical forces. In everyday street interactions, for instance, multilingual individuals often blend languages in ways that defy traditional linguistic boundaries, making translanguaging a natural and ubiquitous phenomenon.

Moreover, the concept of translanguaging has evolved in two primary directions: The "fixed language approach" and the "fluid languaging approach" (Bonacina-Pugh et al., 2021). The fixed language approach, which was prevalent in early translanguaging research, views languages as distinct entities that are alternated in a planned and strategic manner, particularly in educational contexts. On the other hand, the fluid languaging approach, which has gained prominence in recent years, sees translanguaging as a dynamic process where linguistic resources are used flexibly and fluidly, transcending the boundaries of named languages to create a more integrated communicative practice.

This broader understanding of translanguaging emphasizes that it is not confined to structured educational environments but is also a fundamental aspect of how people communicate in their daily lives. As such, translanguaging serves as a practical theory of language that reflects the dynamic, fluid nature of real-world language use, whether in the classroom, at home, or on the street. Grosjean's (1985) *complementarity principle* further complements this framework by highlighting how different aspects of life may require different languages, illustrating the fluid nature of language use in bilinguals' lives.

2.1   TRANSLANGUAGING VS. CODE-SWITCHING: A DISTINCTIVE COMPARISON

In comparing translanguaging and code-switching, it is essential to understand that while both involve the use of multiple languages, they emerge from different theoretical foundations and serve distinct functions within linguistic studies. Code-switching traditionally refers to the practice of alternating between two or more languages or dialects within a conversation or even within a single sentence (Poplack, 1980). This phenomenon has been widely studied in sociolinguistics, where researchers focus on the structural and functional aspects of how and why speakers switch codes in various social contexts. Code-switching is often seen as a reflection of the speaker's ability to shift between different linguistic systems, and it has been analyzed extensively to understand its social, cognitive, and communicative functions (Sun, 2013).

However, code-switching, as understood in traditional linguistic studies, typically operates within the framework of "named languages" (Otheguy et al., 2015)—discrete, bounded systems that speakers switch between. This perspective assumes that speakers are choosing between distinct linguistic codes, each with its own set of grammatical rules and vocabulary. In multilingual communities, for example, speakers might switch from one language to another to mark a change in the social context, such as moving from a casual conversation with friends to a more formal discussion with colleagues. The underlying assumption in code-switching studies is that the act of switching is often a conscious and purposeful activity. Anchimbe (2015) notes that multilingual speakers frequently switch languages to achieve specific communicative goals, such as insulting, warning, or including others, with each choice carrying significant social implications. This reflects the intentional and strategic nature of code-switching, where speakers are fully aware of the meanings and social ramifications associated with their linguistic choices.

On the other hand, translanguaging challenges the very notion of languages as separate, bounded systems. It reflects an insider's perspective, where language is not seen as a collection of distinct codes, but rather as a holistic repertoire of linguistic resources that multilingual individuals draw from seamlessly. Translanguaging scholars argue that multilingual speakers do not mentally compartmentalize their languages but instead use their entire linguistic repertoire fluidly to make meaning and communicate effectively (Otheguy et al., 2015). This insider perspective is fundamentally different from the outsider perspective inherent in code-switching, where language use is observed and categorized externally, often reinforcing the boundaries between named languages.

This difference in perspectives also reflects broader theoretical differences. Code-switching studies often focus on the external social functions of language switching—such as signaling identity, accommodating interlocutors, or managing different cultural contexts—typically from an outsider's viewpoint that views languages as fixed entities. Translanguaging, on the other hand, is concerned with the internal cognitive processes that enable speakers to fluidly utilize their linguistic knowledge. It emphasizes the flexible nature of language use, where speakers are not confined to predefined language systems but rather engage in a continuous process of meaning-making that transcends traditional linguistic boundaries (García & Li, 2014).

Furthermore, translanguaging has been particularly influential in educational contexts, where it has been proposed as a pedagogical practice that leverages students' full linguistic repertoires. Initially, as mentioned in the context of Welsh bilingual education (Williams, 1996), translanguaging was used strategically to enhance learning by allowing students to receive instruction in one language and express their understanding in another. This practice has since expanded, with scholars like García (2009a) advocating for translanguaging as a way to recognize and value the complex linguistic practices of bilingual and multilingual students. By doing so, translanguaging not only supports language learning but also challenges the power dynamics that often marginalize minority languages in educational settings.

In contrast, code-switching has often been viewed within educational contexts as a deviation from the norm, sometimes even being discouraged in favor of promoting proficiency in the dominant language. This reflects a more traditional view of language learning, where the goal is to achieve competence in a particular language, often at the expense of others. However, there is also research that acknowledges that code-switching can play a positive role in language learning, providing cognitive and social benefits that were previously overlooked. For instance, Han et al. (2022) found that bilingual individuals who frequently engage in code-switching demonstrate enhanced cognitive abilities, particularly in cognitive shifting and inhibition. Their study suggests that regular code-switching may help bilinguals maintain focus on their goals and manage conflicting information more effectively, highlighting the cognitive benefits of this practice.

In summary, while both translanguaging and code-switching involve the use of multiple languages, they represent fundamentally different approaches to understanding language use. Code-switching operates within the framework of distinct languages and focuses on how speakers navigate these systems in social contexts. Translanguaging, on the other hand, breaks down the boundaries between languages, emphasizing the integrated and dynamic nature of multilingual language practices. This distinction is crucial for educators, linguists, and policymakers as they consider how best to support and understand the linguistic practices of multilingual individuals.

2.2   EXPLORING THE CORE PREMISES
OF TRANSLANGUAGING THEORY

Translanguaging, as a linguistic phenomenon, is characterized by several fundamental concepts that define its essence:

Flexible language practices: Translanguaging embodies the natural, fluid way in which multilingual individuals engage with their linguistic worlds (see Sánchez, García & Solorza, 2018). It involves the effortless blending of languages, dialects, and non-verbal cues, creating a unique communicative experience that transcends any single language.

Multicompetence: Translanguaging aligns with the concept of multicompetence (Cook, 1991), recognizing that individuals are often competent in multiple languages simultaneously. This challenges the traditional view of monolingual norms and encourages a more inclusive perspective that values and leverages diverse linguistic abilities.

Language as a social practice: Languages are not isolated entities in translanguaging but interconnected resources (see Cenoz & Gorter, 2015). Speakers utilize elements from multiple languages—vocabulary, grammar, idiomatic expressions—as tools to enhance communication, emphasizing meaning over linguistic boundaries.

Linguistic hybridity: Translanguaging celebrates linguistic hybridity, acknowledging and appreciating the unique ways individuals blend languages in their communication (Lankiewicz, 2021). This concept goes beyond the idea of "code-switching" by recognizing the creative and evolving nature of language blending, reflecting the rich linguistic realities experienced by multilingual speakers.

Context-driven communication: Translanguaging is highly responsive to context (see Oliver et al., 2021). Speakers intuitively select linguistic elements based on the situation, audience, and purpose of communication, enriching the message through diverse languages employed.

Cultural embeddedness: Implicit in translanguaging is the recognition that language is intertwined with culture. It emphasizes the cultural context of communication, encouraging individuals to engage with linguistic diversity as well as to appreciate the cultural dimensions embedded in different languages (Tsokalidou & Skourtou, 2020).

Breaking language hierarchies: Translanguaging challenges imposed language hierarchies, valuing all languages equally (see Li & García, 2022). This framework encourages a shift toward viewing all language varieties as legitimate and valuable, even in contexts where certain languages or dialects are traditionally marginalized. While societal biases may persist, translanguaging offers a way to resist these biases by empowering speakers to use their full linguistic resources in more authentic and meaningful ways.

Identity affirmation: Translanguaging recognizes the role of language in shaping personal and cultural identities (Asolati, 2022). It provides a platform for individuals to authentically express their identity through the use of multiple languages, nurturing a deep sense of belonging and empowerment within linguistically diverse communities.

Understanding these core concepts illuminates the depth and richness of translanguaging. It reflects the rich mosaic of linguistic diversity and cultural identity, serving as a guiding principle for effective, inclusive, and culturally sensitive communication. As we explore further, we will analyze the practical applications, historical contexts, and societal implications of translanguaging, uncovering its transformative power in our interconnected world.

REFERENCES

Anchimbe, E. (2015). Code-switching: Between identity and exclusion. In G. Stell & K. Yakpo (Eds.), *Code-switching Between structural and sociolinguistic perspectives* (pp. 117–138). De Gruyter.

Asolati, G. (2022). *Shaping identity through bilingualism and translan- guaging*. (PhD dissertation). https://thesis.unipd.it/retrieve/08e0a6c5- e833-4f8a-80e7-ba44d27319cd/Dissertation%20Giorgia%20Asolati.pdf

Baker, C. (2001, 2011). *Foundations of bilingual education and bilingualism*. Multilingual Matters.

Bonacina-Pugh, F., Da Costa Cabral, I., & Huang, J. (2021). Translanguaging in education. *Language Teaching: Surveys and Studies, 54*(4), 439–471. https:// doi.org/10.1017/S0261444821000173

Cenoz, J., & Gorter, D. (2015). Towards a holistic approach in the study of multilingual education. In J. Cenoz & D. Gorter (Eds.), *Multilingual educa- tion: Between language learning and translanguaging* (pp. 1–15). Cambridge University Press.

Cenoz, J., & Gorter, D. (2017). Minority languages and sustainable translan- guaging: Threat or opportunity? *Journal of Multilingual and Multicultural Development, 38*, 901–912. https://doi.org/10.1080/01434632.2017.128 4855

Creese, A., & Blackledge, A. (2010). Translanguaging in the bilingual classroom: A pedagogy for learning and teaching? *The Modern Language Journal, 94*(1), 103–115. https://doi.org/10.1111/j.1540-4781.2009.00986.x

Cook V. (1991). The poverty-of-the-stimulus argument and multi-competence. *Second Language Research, 7*(2), 103–117. https://www.jstor.org/stable/ 43104425

García, O. (2009a). *Bilingual education in the 21st century: A global perspective*. Wiley-Blackwell.

García, O. (2009b). Education, multilingualism and translanguaging in the 21st century. In T. Skutnabb-Kangas, R. Phillipson, A. Mohanty & M. Panda (Ed.), *Social justice through multilingual education* (pp. 140–158). Multilingual Matters. https://doi.org/10.21832/9781847691910-011

García, O., & Li, W. (2014). *Translanguaging: Language, bilingualism and education*. Palgrave Macmillan.

Grosjean, F. (1985). The bilingual as a competent but specific speaker–hearer. *Journal of Multilingual and Multicultural Development, 6*(6), 467–477. https://doi.org/10.1080/01434632.1985.9994221

Han, X., Li, W., & Filippi, R. (2022). The effects of habitual code-switching in bilingual language production on cognitive control. *Bilingualism: Language and Cognition, 25*(5), 869–889. https://doi.org/10.1017/S13667289220 00244

Lankiewicz, H. A. (2021). Linguistic hybridity and learner identity: translingual practice among plurilinguals in the educational setting. *Czasopismo Polskiego Towarzystwa Neofilologicznego, 56*(1), 55–70. https://doi.org/10.14746/n. 2021.56.1.5

Lewis, G., Jones, B., & Baker, C. (2012a). Translanguaging: Origins and development from school to street and beyond. *Education Research and Evaluation, 18*(7), 641–654. https://doi.org/10.1080/13803611.2012.718488

Lewis, G., Jones, B., & Baker, C. (2012b). Translanguaging: Developing its conceptualisation and contextualisation. *Education Research and Evaluation, 18*(7), 655–670. https://doi.org/10.1080/13803611.2012.718490

Li, W. (2018). Translanguaging as a practical theory of language. *Applied Linguistics, 1*, 9–30. https://doi.org/10.1093/applin/amx039

Li, W., & García, O. (2022). Not a first language but one repertoire: Translanguaging as a decolonizing project. *RELC Journal, 53*(2), 313–324. https://doi.org/10.1177/00336882221092841

Oliver, R., Wigglesworth, G., Angelo, D., & Steele, C. (2021). Translating translanguaging into our classrooms: Possibilities and challenges. *Language Teaching Research, 25*(1), 134–150. https://doi.org/10.1177/136216882 0938822

Otheguy, R., García, O. & Reid, W. (2015). Clarifying translanguaging and deconstructing named languages: A perspective from linguistics. *Applied Linguistics Review, 6*(3), 281–307. https://doi.org/10.1515/applirev-2015-0014

Poplack, S. (1980). Sometimes I'll start a sentence in Spanish y termino en español: Toward a typology of code-switching. *Linguistics, 18*, 581–618. https://doi.org/10.1515/ling.1980.18.7-8.581

Sánchez, M. T., García, O., & Solorza, C. (2018). Reframing language allocation policy in dual language bilingual education. *Bilingual Research Journal, 41*(1), 37–51. https://doi.org/10.1080/15235882.2017.1405098

Sun, M. S. (2013). Code-switching and translanguaging: Potential functions in multilingual classrooms. *Studies in Applied Linguistics & TESOL, 13*(2), 50–52. https://doi.org/10.7916/salt.v13i2.1332

Tsokalidou, R., & Skourtou, E. (2020). Translanguaging as a culturally sustaining pedagogical approach: Bi/Multilingual educators' perspectives. In J. A. Panagiotopoulou, L. Rosen, & J. Strzykala (Eds.), *Inclusion, education and translanguaging* (pp. 219–235). Springer. https://doi.org/10.1007/978-3-658-28128-1_1

Williams, C. (1996). Secondary education: Teaching in the bilingual situation. In C. Williams, G. Lewis, & C. Baker (Eds.), *The language policy: Taking stock* (pp. 39–78). CAI Language Studies Centre.

CHAPTER 3

Historical Overview

Abstract This chapter provides a comprehensive historical overview of translanguaging, tracing its development across different historical and cultural contexts. It explores how translanguaging has been practiced and understood from early multilingual societies through colonial periods to contemporary globalized environments. The chapter begins by examining translanguaging in early multilingual societies, illustrating how diverse linguistic communities engaged in fluid language practices to facilitate communication and cultural exchange. It highlights translanguaging as a natural and adaptive phenomenon rooted in the necessity for effective intercultural interaction. Moving forward, the chapter explores translanguaging in colonial contexts, where linguistic choices were influenced by imperial policies and cultural hegemony. It discusses how translanguaging served as a means of resistance and adaptation among colonized populations, dealing with linguistic hierarchies imposed by colonial powers while preserving cultural and linguistic identities. Furthermore, the chapter investigates translanguaging in postcolonial and globalized contexts, demonstrating its ongoing relevance in a world marked by increased globalization, migration, and digital interconnectedness.

Keywords Historical overview · Translanguaging · Multilingual societies · Colonialism · Postcolonial contexts · Globalization · Linguistic adaptation

© The Author(s), under exclusive license to Springer Nature   19
Switzerland AG 2024
L. M. Pérez Fernández, *Translanguaging in Multicultural Societies*,
https://doi.org/10.1007/978-3-031-74145-6_3

The roots of translanguaging stretch deep into the history of human language use, tracing a path marked by cultural exchanges, migration, and the evolving nature of communication. While the term "translanguaging" itself is relatively modern, the phenomenon it describes has a long and rich history in various societies across the globe.

3.1   Early Multilingual Societies and Translanguaging Practices

To comprehend the roots of translanguaging practices, we journey back through the annals of history, unveiling how ancient civilizations and societies embroiled multilingualism. Early human societies, emerging in diverse geographical locations, invariably encountered linguistic diversity due to migrations, trade, and cultural exchanges. These encounters catalyzed the development of language diversity, laying the foundation for multilingual practices that transcended the confines of individual languages. The study of these early societies is fundamental to understand the essence of translanguaging.

Ancient Mesopotamia: Cradle of Multilingualism

Mesopotamia, often regarded as the cradle of civilization, was home to a myriad of languages including Sumerian, Assyrian, and Babylonian. In this polyglot region, translanguaging was not merely a choice but a necessity. Traders, diplomats, and scholars adeptly crossed linguistic boundaries, employing translanguaging strategies to facilitate communication. Cuneiform inscriptions, which showcase evidence of sustained multilingualism (Crisostomo, 2020), reveal the fluidity with which ancient Mesopotamians transcended linguistic confines, portraying translanguaging as an indispensable tool for survival and prosperity.

The Silk Road: Cultural Crossroads and Multilingual Exchange

The Silk Road, a network of interconnected trade routes that spanned Asia, Europe, and Africa, witnessed a rich amalgamation of cultures and languages. Cities along the Silk Road, particularly the oasis city-states in Central Asia, burgeoned into cosmopolitan centers during the first millennium AD, showcasing remarkable religious, ethnic, and linguistic diversity (Schaefer, 2010). The surge in trade, coupled with

missionary activities, shifting political, religious, and military domina-
tions, and climatic changes, spurred a substantial influx of immigrants
into these urban centers. This demographic shift led to a multilayered
linguistic ecological system marked by the interaction of diverse spoken
and written codes. As a testament to this linguistic diversity, a flourishing written culture emerged, evident in the translation and annotation
of texts and manuscripts in over twenty different languages and various
scripts. Notably, an ecolinguistic study of Tocharian, one of the lesser-
known tongues along the northern route of the Silk Road (Schaefer,
2010), reveals the innovative ways city dwellers coped with communication challenges in multilingual settings. The speakers, coexisting closely
in urban spaces, demonstrated adaptability by changing and developing
their spoken and written codes, giving rise to new linguistic varieties and
registers (Schaefer, 2010). Tocharian itself exhibits traces of the impact of
concurrent codes, both in its lexicon and on the structural, morphological, and morphosyntactic levels. This historical context illustrates how
translanguaging was a practical and necessary phenomenon, reflecting
the adaptability of communication strategies among the varied linguistic
communities traversing this ancient trade route.

The Hellenistic Era: Language as a Unifying Force

In the Hellenistic era, characterized by the spread of Hellenistic culture
and influence following the conquests of Alexander the Great, translanguaging practices flourished as a consequence of vast cultural interactions.
The cities established by Alexander and his successors became vibrant
hubs of diverse ethnicities and languages (see Prnjat, 2019). Notably,
Alexandria in Egypt emerged as a cosmopolitan center, drawing scholars,
traders, and settlers from various regions. This cultural amalgamation
created an environment where diverse linguistic communities engaged in
translanguaging to facilitate communication. The Library of Alexandria,
renowned as a center of learning during this period, featured texts translated and studied in Greek, Latin, Egyptian, and various other languages,
illustrating active translanguaging practices. As scholars and intellectuals
from different linguistic backgrounds converged in the pursuit of knowledge, translanguaging became a practical necessity for sharing ideas and
insights. The city's diverse population, including Greeks, Egyptians, Jews,
and others, further contributed to a linguistic mosaic, where individuals
engaged in the adaptive use of multiple languages for daily interactions,

trade, and intellectual pursuits. This historical context highlights the Hellenistic era as a crucible for translanguaging practices.

Medieval Al-Andalus: Cultural Flourish and Multilingual Expression

In medieval Al-Andalus (711–1492), a unique historical period marked by Islamic rule over the Iberian Peninsula, translanguaging practices thrived as a result of rich cultural interactions among Muslims, Christians, and Jews. The Arab-Muslim rulers established a sophisticated society that valued intellectual pursuits, arts, and sciences, creating an environment conducive to the exchange of ideas across linguistic boundaries. Cities such as Córdoba became renowned centers of learning, attracting scholars from diverse linguistic and cultural backgrounds.

While Al-Andalus was undoubtedly a multilingual society, where languages like Arabic, Romance languages, and Hebrew coexisted, certain contexts saw these languages interact in more dynamic ways. Translanguaging practices emerged as scholars, translators, and everyday people fluidly used multiple languages within the same discourse to meet the demands of communication, learning, and cultural expression. Translation centers in Toledo and Córdoba, for example, played a crucial role in this process (Demir, 2017). Scholars engaged in translating Greek, Roman, and Persian works into Arabic, not only preserving classical knowledge but also facilitating its exchange across linguistic divides. These collaborative efforts of Muslim, Christian, and Jewish translators exemplify how individuals transcended linguistic boundaries for the sake of intellectual enrichment.

Furthermore, individuals from diverse linguistic and religious backgrounds engaged in everyday interactions using multiple languages. Arabic served as the administrative and scholarly language (Gallego, 2003), but individuals proficient in Arabic, Romance languages, and Hebrew often engaged in translanguaging to face the demands of daily life. This fluid use of multiple languages in various social contexts contributed to a rich linguistic mosaic, reflecting the diversity and interconnectedness of the different communities in Al-Andalus.

The literary works produced during this period also demonstrate translanguaging practices. For instance, the "Mozarabic" or "Mudejar" literature, created by Christians living under Muslim rule, often showcased a blending of Arabic and Romance languages (Gómez, 2000). While some of this blending may have been a deliberate artistic choice, it also likely mirrors the natural translanguaging practices of the time, serving as a testament to the linguistic diversity of the region and highlighting the cultural symbiosis that characterized Al-Andalus during this time.

In essence, medieval Al-Andalus stands as a historical example where translanguaging was an integral part of daily life, intellectual pursuits, and cultural expression. The coexistence and interaction of multiple languages and the willingness to engage across linguistic boundaries contributed to the flourishing of a unique society that left a lasting impact on the history of the Iberian Peninsula.

The Renaissance: Revival of Antiquity and Multilingual Creativity

The Renaissance, spanning roughly from the fourteenth to the seventeenth century, was a pivotal period in European history characterized by a revival of interest in classical learning, arts, and sciences. Translanguaging during this era was not merely about switching between languages, but about the flexible and creative use of multiple languages in scholarly, artistic, and diplomatic contexts. Latin, as the language of the Roman Empire and a symbol of classical learning, retained its prominence as the *lingua franca* among scholars. However, alongside Latin, there was a growing appreciation for the vernacular languages, such as Italian, French, Spanish, and English.

One illustrative aspect of translanguaging during the Renaissance is evident in the translation practices of this period, which have made the period be known as the "age of translations" (Hosington, 2015). For instance, Jacques Amyot's translation of Plutarch's *Parallel Lives* exemplifies the Renaissance approach of making classical texts accessible to a broader audience. Amyot meticulously consulted Greek manuscripts to reconstruct Plutarch's text accurately into French, employing strategies like explanatory glosses (e.g., "c'est a dire") to elucidate obscure references for his readers. In contrast, Thomas North's translation of the same work into English reflects a different approach influenced by Puritan beliefs. North's rendition adapts Plutarch's moralizing narratives to resonate more directly with Protestant values, demonstrating how translators during this period faced the dual challenge of remaining faithful to the original texts while also adapting them to contemporary cultural and religious norms. These examples underscore how Renaissance translation practices contributed to the cross-cultural exchange of ideas and knowledge across Europe during this transformative era.

The burgeoning print culture played a pivotal role in the dissemination of knowledge, further contributing to the environment in which translanguaging could thrive. The printing press facilitated the production of books in various languages (Richardson, 2023), leading to a more inclusive intellectual environment. Scholars and authors could now express their ideas in their native languages, enriching the cultural diversity of the Renaissance period. This shift toward vernacular expression was a reflection not just of multilingualism but also of a deeper engagement with the cultural and intellectual possibilities offered by translanguaging.

In the realm of diplomacy, the use of multiple languages was a pragmatic necessity. Ambassadors and diplomats engaged in multilingual exchanges, leveraging their proficiency in various languages to face the challenges of European diplomacy. The ability to adeptly switch between languages became both a diplomatic skill and a manifestation of the interconnected linguistic networks that characterized Renaissance Europe. Moreover, the rise of vernacular literature exemplifies how translanguaging transcended scholarly pursuits. Literary works in languages like Italian (Dante's *Divine Comedy*), Spanish (Cervantes' *Don Quixote*), and English (Shakespeare's plays) showcased a deliberate choice to express ideas and emotions in the language of the people, reflecting a conscious embrace of linguistic diversity.

In essence, translanguaging during the Renaissance was a transformative practice that involved a profound engagement with the cultural, intellectual, and artistic dimensions of language, significantly enriching and interconnecting the various facets of this central period in European history.

3.2   Translanguaging in Colonial Contexts

The advent of colonialism marked a significant juncture in the evolution of translanguaging practices. European colonial powers expanded their empires, encountering diverse linguistic contexts across continents. In these colonial contexts, translanguaging emerged as a key tool, reflecting power dynamics, cultural encounters, and resistance movements.

Colonial Encounters in the Americas

In the Americas, European colonizers encountered indigenous languages and diverse African languages brought by the transatlantic slave trade. While enslaved and indigenous people were often subjected to restrictions on their language use, translanguaging emerged in informal and communal settings where these groups found ways to communicate and adapt to their circumstances. This adaptive linguistic practice involved combining elements of their native languages with European languages, which led to the development of creole languages, where enslaved individuals and indigenous communities incorporated European vocabulary into the grammatical structures of their own languages. These linguistic innovations were not only functional but also expressions of cultural resilience, allowing marginalized groups to preserve elements of their linguistic identity while adapting to their new social environments.

The linguistic divide between colonizers and the diverse populations they encountered frequently necessitated the use of non-verbal communication, including gestures and signs. This reliance on visual and physical cues helped bridge communication gaps where direct language exchange was challenging (Gray & Fiering, 2000).

Moreover, translanguaging was essential in the development of new forms of linguistic expression, such as the Cherokee syllabary created by Sequoyah (Harvey & Rivett, 2017). This writing system, which took inspiration from the Roman alphabet but was adapted to fit the Cherokee language, became a powerful tool for maintaining Cherokee culture and resisting assimilation.

Colonial encounters with Indigenous languages led to the creation of a vast colonial archive of Indigenous language texts. These included Christian didactic texts in various Indigenous languages, legal records, and grammars and vocabularies compiled by missionaries and traders (Harvey & Rivett, 2017). For example, the translation of the Bible into Massachusett in 1663 was a collaborative effort involving the Puritan missionary John Eliot and Indigenous translators like James Printer and Job Nesuton, who played crucial roles in shaping the final text, ensuring that it resonated with the cultural and linguistic context of the Massachusett people.

Nevertheless, translanguaging was not limited to written texts; it also occurred in spoken interactions. Native peoples often used their languages to mediate colonization, adapting old words to new concepts introduced by Europeans. This process allowed them to incorporate new ideas into their existing cultural frameworks. For example, Native communities named European trade goods using their own linguistic terms, which helped them integrate these items into their traditional ways of life.

Translanguaging and Linguistic Hegemony in Africa

During the colonial period in Africa, linguistic interactions reflected the diverse cultures and histories of numerous ethnic groups across the continent. European colonizers, representing nations such as Britain, France, Portugal, Belgium, and others, imposed their languages on African territories for administrative, economic, and cultural purposes. This encounter resulted in a form of translanguaging characterized by the fusion of indigenous African languages with those of the colonizers. Such a process extended beyond mere linguistic borrowing or translation; it often led to the emergence of pidgin and creole languages that became integral to daily communication in colonial settings.

Indigenous African languages, with their rich cultural and historical significance, coexisted with colonial languages in various contexts. Rather than simply borrowing or translating words, translanguaging in this setting involved a more fluid integration of linguistic elements to convey local concepts, expressions, and cultural nuances. This interchange was not a one-sided assimilation but a reciprocal process where both African and European languages influenced each other, resulting in hybrid linguistic forms.

The colonial powers' approaches to language policy varied. In French and Portuguese Africa, the principle of assimilation was prominent. "Natives" were given limited opportunities to learn French and Portuguese, with the goal of transforming them into fully integrated citizens rather than merely colonial subjects (Stroud, 2007). This approach was closely tied to the political stances of the colonial powers. Conversely, British Africa followed a distinct model, influenced by the principles of linguistic colonial management developed in India. In this context, only a limited number of intermediaries in the contact zone were required to be proficient in English, while the general colonized population managed day-to-day affairs through local languages (Stroud, 2007). This approach reflected the different ways in which linguistic policies were adapted based on local contexts and colonial philosophies.

A parallel controversy unfolded in Portuguese Mozambique, echoing the debates in British India. Catholics and Protestants held widely divergent views on the use and development of African languages for educational, administrative, and religious purposes (Stroud, 2007). The divergent views on language policy reflected the challenges of linguistic hegemony, as different colonial powers and religious groups grappled with how to manage the linguistic diversity of the territories they controlled.

The pre-colonial linguistic landscape in Africa, marked by significant multilingualism and cultural confluence, provides important context for understanding these colonial interactions. The ancient kingdom of Mapungubwe, for example, was characterized by a rich tapestry of languages and cultures, with evidence of extensive trade networks that facilitated the use of multiple languages (Makalela, 2016). This historical fluidity and multilingualism highlight the adaptability and resilience of African linguistic practices in the face of colonial impositions.

Furthermore, the concept of "ubuntu" in Southern Africa—meaning "I am because we are"—emphasizes interconnectedness and fluidity (Makalela & Aparecido da Silva, 2023). This philosophy reflects a worldview of interdependence that parallels the translanguaging practices observed in both pre-colonial and colonial Africa (Makalela, 2015). Ubuntu's focus on communal interconnectedness resonates with the fluid nature of language interactions and cultural exchange seen throughout African history.

Translanguaging and Cultural Hybridity in Southeast Asia

Southeast Asia, a region teeming with diverse cultures and languages, witnessed singular translanguaging practices during the colonial period. European powers, such as the British, Dutch, French, and Spanish, grappled with the linguistic challenges across territories encompassing present-day Indonesia, Malaysia, the Philippines, Vietnam, and beyond. Translanguaging in this area involved the interaction between local languages and those of the colonizers, reflecting both the blending of languages and the negotiation of power dynamics.

Each colonial power pursued distinct linguistic policies that reflected their broader colonial philosophies and objectives. These policies ranged from assimilationist strategies that promoted the use of the colonial language among the local elite to more pluralistic approaches that allowed

for the coexistence of local languages alongside the dominant colonial tongue (see Hiroyuki, 2002). In French Indochina, encompassing
present-day Vietnam, Laos, and Cambodia, the French colonial administration promoted the use of French among the educated elite as a
means of cultural assimilation and administrative efficiency (Wang, 2023).
Despite this imposition, Vietnamese intellectuals like Phan Boi Chau and
Nguyen Ai Quoc (later known as Ho Chi Minh) used Vietnamese to
articulate nationalist sentiments and mobilize resistance against colonial
rule.

Conversely, the Dutch East Indies exemplified a context where Dutch
coexisted with Malay and other local languages due to the region's
plurilingual society. When Dutch explorers first arrived in 1596, Malay,
known as the "Italian of the East" for its versatility, was already established as the *lingua franca* across the vast archipelago, spanning cultures,
religions, and numerous indigenous languages (Salverda, 2014). Dutch
colonial policy favored Malay over Dutch due to several reasons. Financial
considerations played a significant role, as did concerns that Dutch would
prove too challenging for Indonesian natives to learn effectively. Additionally, there was apprehension that Dutch, perceived as a "gateway to
the West," could introduce dangerous Western ideas into the archipelago.
The fear was that once Indonesians became proficient in Dutch, they
might engage with literature and ideas considered potentially disruptive or
harmful (Groeneboer, 1998). Consequently, Malay was standardized and
promoted through education and media, bolstering its role in modern-
izing and unifying the archipelago (Salverda, 2014). Meanwhile, Dutch
remained exclusive, taught primarily to Europeans and the elite, reinforcing its status as the language of power within a hierarchical colonial
society in which Indonesian natives were discouraged from using Dutch,
as highlighted in a government circular from 1890 (Groeneboer, 1998).

Similarly, in East Timor, Portuguese colonial rule (circa 1519–1975)
brought about significant linguistic changes, especially in the latter part
of the colonial period when Portugal intensified its policies of social
and linguistic assimilation. Initially, Portuguese influence was limited
to coastal areas and did not deeply penetrate the island's interior.
For much of the seventeenth and eighteenth centuries, Portuguese
was primarily used within the capital, Dili, and among the Fataluku
language community in the far eastern part of Timor, where it func-
tioned as a *lingua franca* (Fox & Babo, 2003). This period of intensified
language policy saw Portuguese enforced in education, administration,

and religious settings, often to the detriment of local languages. Despite this, local languages persisted, and a stable vernacular multilingualism continued throughout Portuguese rule (Hajek, 2002). This situation favored translanguaging practices, where Portuguese and indigenous languages coexisted and influenced each other. For example, contemporary Tetun incorporates many Portuguese loanwords, reflecting a blend of linguistic elements from both languages (Hull, 1999).

In summary, the expansion of European empires brought together diverse linguistic traditions, leading to vibrant interactions and adaptations. The necessity for communication fueled the emergence of translanguaging strategies, encompassing both linguistic exchanges and cultural assimilations and resistances. From the diverse linguistic encounters in the Americas to the reciprocal exchange of languages in Africa and the resilience of Southeast Asian communities, these colonial experiences have left an enduring imprint on language use, policies, and cultural identities.

3.3 TRANSLANGUAGING IN POSTCOLONIAL AND GLOBALIZED CONTEXTS

In the wake of decolonization and globalization, the postcolonial era brought forth a linguistic shift, reshaping translanguaging practices. With the attainment of independence by nations and the growing interconnection of the world, translanguaging underwent an evolution, adjusting to the shifting political, social, and technological environments. This section explores the relationship between translanguaging in postcolonial and globalized contexts, unraveling its ongoing influence on contemporary societies.

Translanguaging and National Identity in Postcolonial Nations

The transition from colonial rule to postcolonial independence marked a profound change in language use, giving rise to complex negotiations surrounding national identity. After gaining independence, nations faced the challenge of determining language policies that met global communication needs while also respecting the diversity of languages spoken within the borders of the newly formed nations.

These challenges became particularly pronounced in the field of education, where the choice of the language of instruction held significant implications. Countries faced dilemmas, such as whether to adopt the language of the former colonizer, establish a multilingual approach or promote the use of indigenous languages. These decisions were intertwined with broader objectives aimed at cultivating unity, inclusivity, and a sense of identity among their diverse populations, shaping the mechanics of teaching and learning accordingly. India exemplifies this, where the decision to adopt Hindi as the official language sparked debates and controversies, leading to the recognition of multiple official languages to accommodate the linguistic diversity present in the nation (Brass, 2005). Similarly, South Africa's post-apartheid education system reflects the difficulties of language choices in the postcolonial era. The apartheid-era South African education system was highly segregated, with students separated based on race and language. White students predominantly received education in their mother tongue, typically English or Afrikaans, while the majority of black students were taught through English, often their second or third language (Gilmartin, 2004). The end of apartheid brought attention to the need for language equity. The 1996 South African Constitution recognized 11 official languages, aiming for equality and the elevation of indigenous languages. However, the practical implementation of language policies was not easy. Subsequent legislative documents diluted the scope for change, with limitations on language choices for learners.

This linguistic negotiation extended into the cultural and artistic spheres. Literary works, films, and other cultural productions became lively platforms for the articulation of national identity. Translanguaging in these creative outlets allowed for the weaving together of diverse linguistic threads to tell stories that captured the richness and challenges of the postcolonial experience. For instance, in postcolonial literature, authors such as Chinua Achebe and Arundhati Roy have employed translanguaging techniques to explore national identity within their contexts. Achebe's (2006) seminal novel *Things Fall Apart* combines Igbo proverbs and phrases with English to illustrate the diverse nature of Nigerian society and challenge colonial narratives of African inferiority. Similarly, Roy's (1997) novel *The God of Small Things* employs a blend of English and Malayalam to evoke the diverse linguistic milieu of Kerala, a state in southern India, and scrutinize power structures within Indian society. As far as cinema is concerned, translanguaging has also been exemplified by films such as Ousmane Sembène's "Xala," which integrates French and Wolof to offer a detailed depiction of Senegalese society and examine the lasting impact of colonialism on African economies.

In the political arena, leaders and policymakers employed official communications and political discourse as main instruments to shape a narrative that acknowledged linguistic diversity while cultivating a shared national identity. The choice of languages in these contexts served as a bridge between the country's historical legacy and its aspirations for a unified future.

However, the journey of translanguaging in postcolonial nations is not without its challenges. Debates and controversies emerge over language hierarchies and the potential marginalization of linguistic minorities. This highlights the ongoing dialogue within these nations, questioning and renegotiating the meaning of belonging in linguistic terms.

Translanguaging in Diaspora Communities

The phenomenon of migration, increasingly propelled by globalization and technological advancements, underscores the profound interconnectedness of societies worldwide. Motivated by aspirations of economic prosperity, safety, and in some cases, fleeing political or religious persecution, individuals embark on journeys to new lands, seeking refuge or better opportunities. As Lambert (2012) notes, the concept of diaspora, originally rooted in biblical narratives and pre-European nomadic traditions, has been revitalized in the twentieth century by the emergence of nation-states, particularly in the Western context. Today, this movement of people encompasses over 200 million individuals, constantly reshaping demographic and cultural patterns.

Migration and diaspora communities brought translanguaging practices to new contexts. Immigrants, refugees, and their descendants often settle in linguistically diverse environments, bringing with them a shared identity, cultural heritage, and a distinct history that sets them apart from the mainstream culture of their host countries (Safran, 1991). In these settings, translanguaging becomes essential for daily interactions, allowing individuals to communicate across linguistic boundaries. Diaspora communities creatively adapt languages, incorporating local dialects and expressions into their speech to facilitate social integration while preserving cultural and linguistic ties to their homelands (Li, 2018).

A study conducted by Iliescu (2017) among Romanian mothers living in Alicante (Spain) sheds light on the fundamental role of language in preserving cultural heritage within immigrant families. Despite residing in a predominantly Spanish-speaking environment, many mothers expressed a steadfast commitment to passing down their native Romanian language to their children, recognizing its significance in shaping their sense of identity and connection to their roots. Additionally, the emergence of phenomena like "rumañol," a hybrid language that combines elements of Romanian and Spanish, commonly spoken within Romanian diaspora communities in Spain, highlights the relationship among diverse linguistic communities and the profound changes migration brings to language usage and cultural identity. Rumañol arises as a creative adaptation to the multicultural environment encountered by diaspora populations, illustrating how migration influences language practices and encourages the formation of new linguistic expressions that reflect the evolving identities of diaspora communities.

Similarly, the United States, with its long history of immigration, exemplifies how translanguaging in diaspora communities is constantly adapting and evolving. From 2016 to 2020, the sociopolitical climate in the United States became particularly harsh for multilingual immigrants from racialized communities, with issues such as family separation, immigration raids, and deportations coming to the fore. Despite the inherent multilingualism of the country, systemic monolingual ideologies often undermine the maintenance and development of multiple languages (Flores & Lewis, 2016). In response to these challenges, Abraham et al. (2021) aimed to investigate how community programs operating outside of school contexts could support the bilingualism of racialized Latinx children in Philadelphia. They collaborated with a bilingual, community-based writing center serving the Latinx community in Philadelphia, where they organized a series of workshops designed to create a translanguaging space. They employed a variety of qualitative research methods, including participatory research and critical/positive discourse analysis. Initial observations revealed that despite the center's bilingual mission, English often dominated communication. Through their research, they discovered that implementing a translanguaging pedagogy within these workshops facilitated the creation of an environment where racialized, emergent bilingual children could fully utilize their linguistic repertoires.

Moreover, literature and artistic expressions within diaspora communities bore the imprints of translanguaging. Authors and artists drew from a repertoire of languages to create narratives that captured the varied experiences of migration (Luo, 2020). Translanguaging, in this context, became a creative endeavor, enriching the cultural array of diaspora expression. In literary works, this often involved authors blending various languages and dialects within their narratives, a technique that allows them to authentically depict the realities of multilingual existence. For example, writers might include dialogues in both the characters' native languages and the dominant language of their new country, thereby illustrating the fluid linguistic boundaries that diasporic individuals encountered daily. This approach enriches character development and mirrors the lived experiences of readers who belong to these communities. Performing arts, including theater and film, also provided rich contexts for translanguaging. Playwrights might write scripts that required actors to switch between languages, reflecting the authentic speech patterns of bilingual or multilingual individuals. This technique brings authenticity to the performance and encourages monolingual audience members to engage with the linguistic diversity portrayed by the characters.

Translanguaging in Digital Spaces

The advent of digital technologies revolutionized communication, expanding the scope of translanguaging into virtual environments. Recent advancements have highlighted transliteration and trans-scripting as significant phenomena in digital spaces. Transliteration, as observed by Angermeyer (2005), involves the use of non-Latin characters, such as Cyrillic or Chinese characters, to represent English-origin items or phrases. Similarly, trans-scripting, as proposed by Spilioti (2019), entails the respelling of words or phrases by creatively manipulating available resources associated with multiple languages and scripts.

In digital spaces, individuals often employ multiple languages with fluidity, blurring the lines between linguistic boundaries. The multifaceted nature of digital communication platforms, ranging from social media to online forums, allows for diverse modes of language use that go beyond monolingual norms. Users leverage various scripts, symbols, and numerals to communicate in innovative ways, challenging conventional norms of written communication (Blommaert, 2012). Social media, in particular, serves as a prominent arena for translanguaging practices, where users routinely incorporate various languages, transliterated expressions, and even emojis to express emotions and ideas.

The collaborative nature of digital spaces fosters a sense of inclusivity and community that transcends linguistic diversity. Online forums, discussion groups, and virtual communities become melting pots of languages, where individuals engage in translanguaging to facilitate understanding and inclusivity (Canagarajah, 2011). Across various digital platforms like social networking sites and multimedia content creation platforms, individuals engage in translanguaging practices to negotiate meaning and express identity within the global digital sphere.

Moreover, digital spaces provide opportunities for the creation and dissemination of digital content that embodies translanguaging. From multilingual blogs to YouTube channels featuring content in various languages, individuals utilize digital platforms to express their identities (Dumrukcic, 2020), share stories, and contribute to the global linguistic tapestry. Thus, moving beyond traditional notions of language boundaries, digital spaces offer a unique arena for linguistic creativity and innovation, where users continually reshape and redefine the contours of communication through translanguaging in its various forms.

Translanguaging and Globalized Economies

In the context of globalized economies, linguistic flexibility plays an important role in shaping communication strategies, facilitating cross-cultural interactions, and influencing business operations (Namatama & Jimaima, 2020). The interconnectedness of global markets demands a linguistic flexibility that transcends traditional language boundaries. As individuals and businesses engage in international trade, negotiations, and collaborations, the use of multiple languages becomes a strategic asset for effective communication and negotiation.

This adaptability is evident in the corporate sphere, particularly in multinational companies dealing with diverse linguistic contexts. Employees and stakeholders from different linguistic backgrounds contribute to a polyglot environment, stimulating innovation and synergy. Translanguaging enables the smooth flow of information, ensuring that language differences do not impede the exchange of ideas and expertise.

Furthermore, the use of translanguaging in globalized economies extends beyond spoken and written communication. Visual and symbolic elements, such as multilingual signage, branding, and digital content, contribute to a multilingual corporate identity. This practice reflects an acknowledgment of linguistic diversity as an integral part of global market engagement.

The importance of linguistic adaptability in globalized economies is also prominent in digital communication platforms. Online business transactions, virtual meetings, and e-commerce platforms often involve the use of multiple languages to cater to a diverse customer base. The digital space becomes a dynamic arena where businesses engage with consumers through language choices that resonate with their cultural and linguistic preferences.

In conclusion, the linguistic contexts of colonial and postcolonial eras provided a foundational backdrop for the development of translanguaging practices. Although direct evidence of translanguaging from these periods may be limited, the historical interplay of languages and the relationship among power and identity set the stage for the evolution of translanguaging as a significant phenomenon in contemporary linguistic environments.

REFERENCES

Abraham, S., Kedley, K., Fall, M., Krishnarmurthy, S., & Tulino, D. (2021). Creating a translanguaging space in a bilingual community-based writing program. *International Multilingual Research Journal, 15*(3), 211–234. https://doi.org/10.1080/19313152.2021.1883791

Achebe, C. (2006). *Things fall apart.* Penguin Classics.

Angermeyer, P. S. (2005). Spelling bilingualism: Script choice in Russian American classified ads and signage. *Language in Society, 34*(4), 493–531. https://doi.org/10.1017/S0047404505050190

Blommaert, J. (2012). Supervernaculars and their dialects. *Dutch Journal of Applied Linguistics, 1*(1), 1–14. https://doi.org/10.1075/dujal.1.1.03blo

Brass, P. R. (2005). *Language, religion, and politics in North India.* iUniverse.

Canagarajah, S. (2011). Translanguaging in the classroom: Emerging issues for research and pedagogy. *Applied Linguistics Review, 2*, 1–28. https://doi.org/10.1515/9783110239331.1

Crisostomo, C. J. (2020). Sumerian and Akkadian language contact. In R. Hasselbach-Andee (Ed.), *A companion to ancient near Eastern languages* (pp. 401–420). Wiley-Blackwell.

Demir, M. (2017). The translation activities of Andalus period. *European Journal of Literature, Language and Linguistic Studies, 1*(1), 13–23. https://doi.org/10.5281/zenodo.837843

Dumrukcic, N. (2020). Translanguaging in social media. Output for FLT didactics. *HeiEducation Journal, 5*, 109–137. https://doi.org/10.17885/heiup.heied.2020.5

Flores, N., & Lewis, M. (2016). From truncated to sociopolitical emergence: A critique of super-diversity in sociolinguistics. *International Journal of the Sociology of Language, 241*, 97–124. https://doi.org/10.1515/ijsl-2016-0024

Fox, J. J., & Babo Soares, D. (2003). *Out of the Ashes: Destruction and reconstruction of East Timor.* ANU Press. https://doi.org/10.26530/oapen_459402

Gallego, M. A. (2003). The languages of Medieval Iberia and their religious dimension. *Medieval Encounters, 9*(1), 107–139.

Gilmartin, M. (2004). Language, education and the New South Africa. *Tijdschrift Voor Economische En Sociale Geografie, 95*(4), 405–418.

Gómez, M. M. (2000). La lengua "aljamiada" y su literatura: una variante islámica del español. *Castilla: Estudios de literatura,* 25, 71–83

Gray, E. G., & Fiering, N. (2000). *The language encounter in the Americas, 1492–1800.* Berghahn Books.

Groeneboer, K. (1998). *Gateway to the West. The Dutch language in Colonial Indonesia 1600–1950. A history of language policy.* Amsterdam University Press.

Hajek, J. (2002). *Language maintenance and survival in East Timor: All change now?* Routledge.

Harvey, S. P., & Rivett, S. (2017). Colonial-Indigenous language encounters in North America and the intellectual history of the Atlantic World. *Early American Studies: An Interdisciplinary Journal, 15*(3), 442–473. https://doi.org/10.1353/eam.2017.0017

Hiroyuki, M. (2002). *Colonial language policies and their effects.* World Congress on Language Policies. Barcelona 16–20 April. https://www.linguapax.org/wp-content/uploads/2015/07/CMPL2002_T1_MHiroyuki.pdf

Hosington, B. M. (2015). Introduction: Translation and print culture in early modern Europe. *Renaissance Studies, 29*(1), 5–18. http://www.jstor.org/stable/26631746

Hull, G. (1999). *Standard Tetum – English dictionary.* Allen & Unwin.

Iliescu, C. (2017). Arguments for a translanguaging approach to the case of Romanian Diaspora in Spain. *Philologica Jassyensia, 2*(26), 281–293.

Lambert, J. (2012). In place of foreword. In C. Iliescu Gheorghiu (Cord.), *Traducción y (a)culturación en la era global* (pp. 9–10). Agua Clara.

Li, W. (2018). Translanguaging as a practical theory of language. *Applied Linguistics, 1,* 9–30. https://doi.org/10.1093/applin/amx039

Luo, X. (2020). Translation and diaspora literature. *Asia Pacific Translation and Intercultural Studies, 7*(1), 1–2. https://doi.org/10.1080/23306343.2020.1748796

Makalela, L. (2015). Moving out of linguistic boxes: The effects of translanguaging strategies for multilingual classrooms. *Language and Education, 29*(3), 200–2017. https://doi.org/10.1080/09500782.2014.994524

Makalela, L. (2016). Ubuntu translanguaging: An alternative framework for complex multilingual encounters. *Southern African Linguistics and Applied*

Language Studies, *34*(3), 187–196. https://doi.org/10.2989/16073614.2016.1250350

Makalela, L., & Aparecido da Silva, K. (2023). Ubuntu translanguaging: A decolonial model for the global south multilingualism. *Revista Linguagem & Ensino*, *26*(1), 84–97. https://doi.org/10.15210/rle.v26i1.6804

Namatama, K. B., & Jimaima, H. (2020). Translanguaging as commodified semiotic resource among traders and customers of Soweto Market in Lusaka Zambia. *Multidisciplinary Journal of Language and Social Sciences Education*, *3*(2), 229–249.

Prnjat, D. (2019). Culture and communication: A look at the Hellenistic Mediterranean. In D. K. Vukcevic & P. Rudan (Eds.), *MASA-EMAN Symposium. culture, technology and humanism*. Montenegrin Academy of Sciences and Arts.

Richardson, B. (2023). Multilingual Printing. In A. Petrocchi & J. Brown (Eds.), *Languages and cross-cultural exchanges in renaissance Italy* (pp. 35–64). Brepols Publishers.

Roy, A. (1997). *The god of small things*. Thorndike.

Safran, W. (1991). Diasporas in modern societies: Myths of homeland and return. *Diaspora: A Journal of Transnational Studies*, *1*(1), 83–99.

Salverda, R. (2014). Between Dutch and Indonesian: Colonial Dutch in time and space. In F. Hinskens & J. Taeldeman (Ed.), *Volume 3 Dutch* (pp. 800–821). De Gruyter Mouton. https://doi.org/10.1515/9783110261332.800

Schaefer, C. (2010). Multilingualism and language contact in urban centres along the Silk Road during the first millennium AD. In P. J. J. Sinclair, G. Nordquist, F. Herschend, & C. Isendahl (Eds.), *The urban mind: Cultural and Environmental dynamics* (pp. 441–455). Uppsala University.

Spilioti, T. (2019). From transliteration to trans-scripting: Creativity and multilingual writing on the internet. *Discourse, Context & Media*, *29*, 1–10. https://doi.org/10.1016/j.dcm.2019.03.001

Stroud, C. (2007). 21. Multilingualism in ex-colonial countries. In P. Auer & L. Li (Ed.), *Handbook of multilingualism and multilingual communication* (pp. 509–538). De Gruyter Mouton. https://doi.org/10.1515/9783110198553.4.509

Wang, R. (2023). An analysis of the influence of French colonization on the Vietnamese education system. *Interdisciplinary Humanities and Communication Studies*, *1*(1), 1–14. https://doi.org/10.61173/aj42qn74

CHAPTER 4

Language Policies and Their Impact on Translanguaging Practices

Abstract Focusing on the intersection of language policies and translanguaging, this chapter explores how governmental decisions, institutional frameworks, and educational systems significantly influence the manifestation and evolution of translanguaging in diverse societal contexts. The chapter begins by examining the impact of government-led language frameworks. It highlights how official language policies shape the linguistic landscape of nations, often favoring certain languages while marginalizing others. For instance, in postcolonial settings like many African nations, the historical imposition of English or French as official languages continues to influence translanguaging practices, affecting everyday communication and cultural identities. Furthermore, the chapter explores non-governmental approaches to language policies emphasizing the key role of community organizations, advocacy groups, and international bodies in promoting linguistic diversity and supporting translanguaging. Educational systems and language instruction constitute another focal point of the chapter. It examines how educational policies impact language choices within schools, the recognition of linguistic diversity, and the adoption of translanguaging practices. The chapter underscores the challenges and opportunities in integrating translanguaging into educational settings, emphasizing the need for inclusive pedagogies that value students' linguistic repertoires.

© The Author(s), under exclusive license to Springer Nature Switzerland AG 2024
L. M. Pérez Fernández, *Translanguaging in Multicultural Societies*,
https://doi.org/10.1007/978-3-031-74145-6_4

Keywords Language policies · Translanguaging · Linguistic diversity · Educational systems · Cultural identity · Inclusive pedagogies

The intersection of language policies and translanguaging practices is paramount for understanding how communication, identity, and societal structures interact. This section explores the impact of language policies on the manifestation and evolution of translanguaging, emphasizing the role of governmental decisions, institutional frameworks, and educational systems.

4.1   GOVERNMENT-LED LANGUAGE FRAMEWORKS

Government-led language frameworks wield significant influence over the linguistic diversity of a nation, often acting as a catalyst or impediment to translanguaging practices. As we saw in the previous chapter, governmental decisions regarding official languages are often deeply rooted in historical contexts. For instance, the establishment of English as the official language in postcolonial nations reflects historical ties with former colonial powers. This historical context, while shaping national identity, also influences translanguaging practices. In several African nations, the colonial legacy of English or French as official languages persists. This historical continuity influences how these languages are interwoven with indigenous languages in everyday communication, illustrating the nature of postcolonial translanguaging.

Governments face a wide range of challenges when devising language policies, often balancing the promotion of linguistic diversity with the preference for a dominant language. This preference significantly affects everyday communication. In Spain, where regional languages like Catalan, Galician, and Basque coexist with Spanish, government efforts to preserve and promote linguistic diversity have been manifested through policies supporting these regional languages. These measures include funding for language education programs, cultural initiatives, and media content in these languages. Additionally, there are legal provisions that recognize the official status of these languages in their respective regions, ensuring their use in governmental institutions, education, and public services. Despite official recognition, these languages face hurdles, and the prevalence of Spanish in mainstream media and official documents reinforces its societal dominance. A parallel situation occurs in various Indian states, where Hindi, as a dominant language, can overshadow regional languages, influencing communication in public spaces and government institutions. The repercussions of this linguistic favoritism are evident in the prioritization of Hindi in official communication, potentially sidelining the rich linguistic diversity that characterizes the nation. Moreover, the preference for a dominant language in official settings may limit access to economic opportunities for speakers of minority languages. For instance, in regions where indigenous languages coexist with a dominant language, economic activities tied to the dominant language can inadvertently disadvantage speakers of minority languages, affecting employment prospects and entrepreneurship.

Balancing the promotion of linguistic diversity with the dominance of a particular language requires governments to implement initiatives that support varied language usage. In diverse countries like the United States, where the range of languages spoken is wide and growing, the impact on daily interactions and translanguaging practices is significant. In urban centers such as Los Angeles, Miami, and New York, Spanish has become more than just a secondary language; it is increasingly prevalent in public spaces, including shops, restaurants, and public transport. This presence of Spanish influences cultural norms and societal interactions beyond immigrant communities. Governmental responses to this linguistic diversity vary, with some states and municipalities implementing policies and programs to reflect an understanding of the natural, fluid nature of language use, such as bilingual signage in public spaces, multilingual education programs in schools, and initiatives for language revitalization. These efforts aim to support and acknowledge the diverse linguistic practices that emerge in everyday life. Similarly, private companies like Walmart and Home Depot have adopted bilingual in-store signage (Mantel & Kellaris, 2023) as a means of accommodating diverse linguistic communities and promoting accessibility. These practices, while structured, resonate with the spontaneous and natural ways people blend languages in their interactions.

In Latin America, the recognition of indigenous languages varies among countries. Bolivia and Paraguay, for instance, have declared multiple indigenous languages as official languages alongside Spanish, reflecting a commitment to linguistic diversity at the national level. Bolivia's constitution explicitly acknowledges all indigenous languages as official, while Paraguay designates both Spanish and Guarani with certain restrictions on Guarani's official use (Zajícová, 2017). Other indigenous languages in Paraguay are recognized solely as part of the cultural heritage, resembling the legal status of indigenous languages in Costa Rica or El Salvador. In Nicaragua, Ecuador, and Peru, indigenous languages receive official status at the national level, but with hierarchical arrangements based on territorial or demographic factors. In Nicaragua, the official use of indigenous languages is limited to the Autonomous Regions, while in Ecuador, ancestral languages are officially recognized for indigenous peoples in their inhabited areas, alongside Spanish. Similarly, Peru designates Quechua, Aimara, and other indigenous languages as official in areas where they predominate (Zajícová, 2017). Mexico takes a unique approach by not declaring any official language nationally but recognizing indigenous languages and Spanish as national languages with equal validity in their respective contexts. Meanwhile, Venezuela mandates the official use of indigenous languages for indigenous communities, ensuring respect throughout the country. While these countries share a commitment to recognizing and protecting indigenous languages, there may be variations in the specific details of their legislative frameworks and implementation strategies. Factors such as regional circumstances, historical context, and government initiatives can influence the effectiveness of language policies in promoting linguistic diversity and preserving indigenous cultures. However, there are countries where the linguistic situation hasn't required specific legislation as indigenous languages disappeared long ago. Examples include Cuba, the Dominican Republic, Uruguay, or Puerto Rico, the latter being a special case as it has two official languages, Spanish and English.

China presents a unique case with its language policies, reflecting the country's vast linguistic diversity. The country's minority language policies have undergone significant changes over the decades, reflecting broader political and social transformations. In the early and mid-1950s, the Chinese government actively supported minority languages, establishing autonomous regions, creating writing systems for minority languages, and training officials in these languages. However, during the late 1950s and the Cultural Revolution (1966–1976), the focus shifted toward assimilation, with Mandarin Chinese being enforced as the medium of instruction in schools within minority regions (Wang & Phillion, 2009). Since the late 1970s, there has been a formal reinstatement of minority language rights, as evidenced by the 1982 Constitution and the 1984 PRC Regional Autonomy Law for Minority Nationalities, which mandate the protection of minority languages and cultures. Despite these legal protections, significant gaps exist between policy and practice. Factors such as poverty, a lack of qualified bilingual teachers, or prejudice against minority languages (Wang & Phillion, 2009) hinder effective implementation. The dominance of Mandarin Chinese, driven by national unity and economic opportunities, further exacerbates the marginalization of minority languages. Consequently, these minority languages face endangerment and minority students often experience higher dropout and illiteracy rates. The discrepancies between official policies and their enactment underscore the challenges in balancing national unity with the preservation of linguistic and cultural diversity in China.

Another notable example is Canada, a country renowned for its commitment to bilingualism and multiculturalism. The cornerstone of Canada's language policy is the Official Languages Act, first enacted in 1969 and subsequently updated. This legislation guarantees the rights of all Canadians to access federal services in both English and French and mandates that federal institutions promote the use of both languages. Through initiatives such as the Action Plan for Official Languages, the government provides funding and resources to promote bilingualism in education, government services, and the public sphere. In the education sector, Canada has implemented numerous programs to support bilingual and multilingual education. Immersion programs, where students are taught in their second official language, are a prominent feature of the Canadian educational domain. Moreover, recognizing the importance of Indigenous languages, the Canadian government has implemented the Indigenous Languages Component (Government of Canada, 2024). This initiative supports the efforts of Indigenous communities and organizations to reclaim, revitalize, maintain, and strengthen Indigenous languages. With a distinction-based funding approach, First Nations, Inuit, and the Métis Nation work with the Department of Canadian Heritage to implement their own language revitalization strategies. However, despite these efforts, challenges remain. The implementation of bilingual and multilingual education policies varies across provinces and territories, reflecting regional differences and local priorities. There are also ongoing debates about the best methods to support immigrant languages and the revitalization of Indigenous languages.

Another context worth mentioning is Singapore, where the dominance of English in various domains and public discourse, as noted by

Quentin (2011), exemplifies how government language policies can shape language use and translanguaging practices in everyday life. Singapore is renowned for its rich linguistic diversity, stemming from its history as an immigrant society and from a linguistic perspective. Officially, the country recognizes four languages: English, Mandarin, Tamil, and Malay (reflecting the major ethnic groups within the population) with Malay also serving as the national language. Additionally, a plethora of other languages thrive within Singaporean communities (Ng & Cavallaro, 2021).

According to Ng and Cavallaro (2021), two main policies have shaped Singapore's linguistic landscape: The Bilingual Policy introduced in 1966 and the Speak Mandarin Campaign (SMC) launched in 1979. The Bilingual Policy emphasized English-plus bilingualism, making English the primary medium of instruction in schools and for formal contexts. This policy aimed to equip Singaporeans for global economic engagement while maintaining ethnic languages like Mandarin, Malay, and Tamil as second languages in education. Consequently, the dominance of English has significantly increased in various domains and public discourse, impacting everyday interactions and translanguaging practices (Quentin, 2011). The Speak Mandarin Campaign promoted Mandarin over other Chinese languages, aiming to unify the Chinese community linguistically and culturally (Ng & Cavallaro, 2021). Consequently, these laws "elevated English and Mandarin to the status of majority languages, and relegated other Chinese vernaculars, Malay, and Tamil to the rank of minority languages" (Ng & Cavallaro, 2021, p. 150).

When exploring the impact of government-led language frameworks, it becomes clear that the nature of translanguaging is deeply intertwined with historical, sociocultural, and legal dimensions. Government decisions regarding official languages shape both national identity and the daily practices and expressions of linguistic communities. This relationship between language policies and translanguaging practices underscores the need for policies that are sensitive to the diverse linguistic contexts within postcolonial nations.

4.2   Non-Government Approaches

While governmental frameworks indeed wield considerable influence over language policies, it is essential to recognize the significant contributions of other influential actors in shaping and supporting plurilingual practices that might include translanguaging. Community organizations, advocacy groups, and international bodies are essential for advancing the promotion of linguistic diversity and creating conducive environments where translanguaging can thrive.

Non-governmental organizations (NGOs) and initiatives worldwide are instrumental in language advocacy, preservation, and promotion. For instance, the *Endangered Languages Project* and the *Linguistic Society of America* actively work to raise awareness about endangered languages and support revitalization efforts. Such initiatives are vital as they create a supportive environment for multilingualism and translanguaging and, thus, contribute significantly to maintain linguistic diversity.

The *Endangered Languages Project*, for example, is a collaborative platform developed through a partnership between Google and the Alliance for Linguistic Diversity. It serves as a centralized online space where researchers, linguists, and language communities can come together to share knowledge, resources, and documentation efforts aimed at preserving endangered languages. One of the key features of the *Endangered Languages Project* is its interactive map, which allows users to explore the geographic distribution of endangered languages worldwide. Through this map, users can access detailed information about specific languages, including their endangerment status, linguistic classification, and available documentation resources. Additionally, the project hosts a variety of tools and resources for language documentation and revitalization, including language documentation kits, training materials, and guidelines for community-based language revitalization projects.

Likewise, the *Linguistic Society of America* (LSA) promotes the study and preservation of diverse languages. Through advocacy efforts, the LSA works to raise awareness about the importance of linguistic diversity and the need to protect endangered languages, such as indigenous languages spoken by Native American communities like the Cherokee and Navajo languages. Additionally, the society facilitates educational initiatives aimed at promoting an appreciation for linguistic diversity among both scholars and the general public. Furthermore, the LSA provides financial support for linguistic research endeavors, including projects focused on language documentation, revitalization, and the exploration of translanguaging practices within minority language communities.

One key aspect of these NGOs' work is their focus on community-driven initiatives. Community organizations, grassroots movements, and cultural centers often spearhead efforts to preserve and promote

languages at risk of extinction or marginalization within broader societal contexts. These initiatives are crucial in fostering linguistic diversity
and supporting translanguaging practices in different communities. For
instance, the Maori community in New Zealand has established language
nests, known as "kohanga reo," where children are immersed in the Maori
language alongside English from a young age (Maia et al., 2018). These
community-driven initiatives aim to revitalize the Maori language while
embracing translanguaging as a natural part of language acquisition and
communication.

Similarly, the *New York Immigration Coalition* (NYIC) plays a central
part in expanding language access and advocating for the rights of New
York's diverse immigrant communities. New York State has one of the
largest immigrant populations in the nation, with over 5.7 million New
Yorkers speaking a language other than English at home. Despite the
enactment of a statewide Language Access policy, interpretation and
translation services remain inconsistent, particularly at the county level.
The NYIC's 2024 State Priorities highlight the urgent need for more
robust language services, including the development of a bilingual workforce and the expansion of language access to regional areas. Their efforts
aim to ensure that non-English speakers can access critical services and
information in their preferred languages, thus supporting multilingual
communication within the community. For instance, the NYIC promotes
initiatives that facilitate the integration of multiple languages in public
services, education, and everyday interactions. These initiatives enable
immigrant communities to maintain their native languages while learning
and using English, thereby encouraging translanguaging practices that
enhance communication, social integration, and cultural preservation.

Another key organization in advancing language education in Europe
is the European Centre for Modern Languages (ECML), based in Graz,
Austria. As a Council of Europe institution, the ECML is dedicated to
promoting a structured and systematic plurilingual approach to language
education. Their initiatives focus on developing organized frameworks
that integrate multiple languages into educational settings, aiming to
enhance linguistic competencies and foster inclusive learning environments. While the ECML emphasizes formal methodologies for language
integration, such as well-defined curricular frameworks and structured
educational practices, these approaches can also create a supportive environment for translanguaging. By establishing a solid foundation for

plurilingual education, the ECML's frameworks facilitate the incorporation of diverse linguistic resources in a way that can complement and
support translanguaging practices. The ECML organizes workshops and
conferences that bring together educators, policymakers, and researchers
to exchange best practices and develop new strategies for language
teaching that embrace multilingualism. One such initiative, spanning from
2011 to 2013, was the "Quality Education in Romani for Europe"
(QualiRom) project. This initiative was dedicated to promoting the integration of Romani into education systems and empowering Romani
speakers. With a focus on enhancing literacy levels in Romani and
offering specialized training for Romani language instructors, QualiRom
exemplified the ECML's dedication to establishing inclusive education
environments and preserving minority languages.

In essence, non-governmental organizations are fundamental actors
in promoting linguistic diversity worldwide. Through advocacy, support
for language revitalization, and the creation of inclusive education environments, these entities contribute significantly to preserving cultural
heritage and promoting multilingualism. Their efforts highlight the
importance of embracing linguistic diversity as integral to human identity
and cultural expression, contributing to more inclusive and harmonious
societies.

4.3 EDUCATIONAL SYSTEMS
AND LANGUAGE INSTRUCTION

Educational systems establish the foundations of language instruction
by determining the languages of instruction, the inclusion of additional languages in the curriculum, and the recognition of linguistic
diversity among students. In multilingual countries like India, language
policies often impact the choices made in educational settings. For
example, the Three-Language Formula in India encourages the teaching
of students' mother tongue (the regional language), Hindi (or another
Indian language in Hindi-speaking areas), and English (Ray et al., 2023).
Similarly, in Spain, which comprises multiple autonomous communities, educational policies aim to balance the promotion of regional
languages with the proficiency of Spanish and, in schools with bilingual programs, a third language, normally English, reflecting the diverse
sociolinguistic context of the country (Gorter & Cenoz, 2015). The coexistence of these languages in education necessitates careful consideration

of linguistic rights, curriculum design, and teacher training to ensure effective language instruction.

The curricular choices made within educational systems contribute to the establishment of language hierarchies. In some cases, the dominance of one language over others can be reinforced through curriculum design. For instance, in South Africa, where the post-apartheid education system aims for linguistic equity, challenges persist. English, often considered a language of privilege, may still influence curricular choices, perpetuating language hierarchies and impacting translanguaging practices. Sometimes, the challenges faced in educational systems can be diverse, encompassing both linguistic and political dimensions, as in the case of Spain, where the recognition and promotion of regional languages in education often intersect with broader discussions on cultural identity and autonomy.

As educational paradigms shift, the promotion of effective translanguaging practices within diverse learning environments faces numerous hurdles. One significant obstacle is the resistance to recognizing and valuing translanguaging as a legitimate pedagogical approach. In many educational systems, there is a tendency to adhere strictly to monolingual norms (Duarte & Kirsch, 2020), hindering the organic use of multiple languages for effective learning. Overcoming these challenges requires a paradigm shift that acknowledges the linguistic resources students bring to the learning environment. In countries or regions with multiple official languages, legislative decisions can impact language policies in schools. For instance, in Canada, the Official Languages Act ensures that English and French have equal status in federal institutions. However, the interpretation and implementation of these laws may vary, influencing the extent to which translanguaging is accepted and supported in educational settings.

Amid these challenges, the transformative potential of translanguaging in educational systems becomes evident. Translanguaging is key to inclusive pedagogy by recognizing and valuing the linguistic diversity of students. Inclusive language policies create an environment where students feel empowered to use their full linguistic repertoire for learning. For example, the inclusion of indigenous languages in the curriculum in New Zealand, such as the Māori language, reflects the country's commitment to acknowledging the significance of its diverse linguistic heritage (Fithri, 2019). This commitment aligns with the government's approved Maori language policy objectives, including enhancing the number of Māori speakers, improving proficiency, providing opportunities for language use, and encouraging positive attitudes toward Māori/ English bilingualism.

The implementation of translanguaging practices requires a holistic approach that encompasses teacher training and ongoing professional development (Fang et al., 2022). Teachers need support to understand the principles of translanguaging, develop strategies for integrating multiple languages in the classroom, and address the challenges associated with diverse linguistic backgrounds among students. Investments in teacher training contribute to the successful adoption of translanguaging in educational settings.

Moreover, integrating translanguaging practices in education involves active engagement with parents and communities (Bautista-Thomas, 2015). Transparent communication about the benefits of translanguaging, dispelling misconceptions, and involving parents in their children's language learning journey can create a supportive environment. Community engagement ensures that language policies align with the linguistic needs and aspirations of the local population.

The contemporary integration of technology in education provides unprecedented opportunities to enhance translanguaging practices. In today's digital age, various technological tools and platforms offer a lively space for promoting linguistic diversity within educational settings. Online resources, language learning apps, and virtual classrooms create a collaborative environment where students can easily use several languages. For instance, multimedia presentations, interactive language learning applications, and digital content can cater to diverse language proficiencies, allowing students to engage with educational materials in their preferred language.

As far as assessment in translanguaging practices is concerned, educational systems need to evolve their traditional strategies. Traditional assessment methods may not fully capture the multilingual proficiency of students engaged in translanguaging practices. Therefore, there is a growing need for the development of innovative assessment methods that can accommodate the varied ways in which languages are utilized across different settings and by diverse populations. Portfolios, project-based assessments, and collaborative tasks can provide a more comprehensive view of students' language abilities in diverse contexts.

Expanding the scope to a global perspective, educational systems are increasingly embracing global collaborations and interconnected learning.

Institutions recognize the significance of preparing students for a world that is more interconnected than ever before, actively participating in collaborative projects with counterparts from diverse countries. This approach exposes students to a wide array of languages and encourages the use of translanguaging in cross-cultural educational initiatives.

Simultaneously, advocacy for linguistic rights is taking a center stage as a transformative dimension in shaping educational systems. Ongoing efforts aim to ensure that students have the right to learn and use their native languages, nurturing an inclusive educational environment. Educational policies focused on linguistic rights contribute significantly to the acknowledgment and celebration of linguistic diversity, promoting an atmosphere where translanguaging is both accepted but also actively encouraged.

The evolution of educational strategies encompasses the embrace of multimodal learning environments. Going beyond the confines of traditional classroom settings, educational systems are integrating diverse modes of learning, including visual aids, interactive activities, and immersive experiences, to facilitate and enhance translanguaging practices. Recognizing the diverse preferences of students in their learning approaches, this multimodal shift enriches the effectiveness of translanguaging practices.

In an era that values cultural competence, educational systems are placing a greater emphasis on intercultural communication. Translanguaging involves not just language use but also understanding the cultural nuances embedded in communication. Cultivating cultural competence through language instruction ensures that students speak multiple languages and engage skillfully with the cultural richness inherent in diverse linguistic expressions.

To further support translanguaging, educational systems are adopting more flexible curriculum designs. The acknowledgment that rigid structures can impede the organic use of multiple languages underscores the importance of curriculum flexibility. This adaptability empowers educators to seamlessly incorporate translanguaging practices, catering to the varied linguistic needs inherent in diverse student populations. Ultimately, the fluidity of flexible curriculum design becomes indispensable in creating an environment where translanguaging can naturally flourish.

REFERENCES

Bautista-Thomas, C. M. (2015). Translanguaging and parental engagement. *Theory, Research and Action in Urban Education*, 4(1). https://traue. commons.gc.cuny.edu/volume-iv-issue-1-fall-2015/translanguaging-and-par ental-engagement/

Cenoz, J., & Gorter, D. (2015). Towards a holistic approach in the study of multilingual education. In J. Cenoz & D. Gorter (Eds.), *Multilingual education: Between language learning and translanguaging* (pp. 1–15). Cambridge University Press.

Duarte, J., & Kirsch, C. (2020). Introduction: Multilingual approaches for teaching and learning. In C. Kirsch & J. Duarte (Eds.), *Multilingual approaches for teaching and learning: from acknowledging to capitalising on multilingualism in European mainstream education* (pp. 17–27). Routledge. https://doi.org/10.4324/9780429059674-1

Fang, F., Zhang, L. J., & Sah, P. K. (2022). Translanguaging in language teaching and learning: Current practices and future directions. *RELC Journal*, 53(2), 305–312. https://doi.org/10.1177/00336882221114478

Fithri, S. (2019). An overview of indigenous language programs in Australian and New Zealand. *Advances in Social Science, Education and Humanities Research*, volume 254, Eleventh Conference on Applied Linguistics (CONAPLIN 2018), 250–254.

Government of Canada. (2024). *Indigenous Languages and Cultures Program*. https://www.canada.ca/en/canadian-heritage/services/funding/aboriginal-peoples.html

Maia, M., Nascimento, M., & Whan, C. (2018). The Maori language nest program: Voices of language and culture revitalization in Aotearoa, New Zealand. *Ecolingüística: Revista Brasileira de Ecologia e Linguagem*, 4(1), 108–127.

Mantel, S., & Kellaris, J. (2023). Bilingual signs: How language influences shoppers. *Interdisciplinary Journal of Signage and Wayfinding*, 7(1), 5–20.

Ng, B. C., & Cavallaro, F. (2021). Where have all my languages gone? Aging and the changing multilingual linguistic ecology. In R. Blackwood & U. Røyneland (Eds.), *Trajectories of language: policies, spaces and interactions. Volume I: Multilingualism Across the Lifespan*, (pp. 147–168). Routledge. https://doi.org/10.4324/9781003125815-7

Ray, A., Sarangi, P., Purohit, B., & Dash, S. R. (2023). Three language formula in national education policy, 2020 of India: From the Stakeholder's perspectives. *Journal of Higher Education Theory and Practice*, 23(13), 136–154. https://doi.org/10.33423/jhetp.v23i13.6369

Wang, Y., & Phillion, J. (2009). Minority language policy and practice in China: The need for multicultural education. *International Journal of Multicultural Education*, 11(1), 1–14. https://doi.org/10.18251/ijme.v11i1.138

Zajícová, L. (2017). Lenguas indígenas en la legislación de los países hispanoamericanos. *O nomázein: Revista de lingüística, filología y traducción de la Pontificia Universidad Católica de Chile*, Special Issue 3, 171–203.

PART II

Theoretical Foundations

CHAPTER 5

Sociolinguistic Theories and Translanguaging

Abstract This chapter explores the relationship between sociolinguistic theories and translanguaging practices, highlighting how language variation, social identity, and power dynamics intersect within diverse multilingual contexts. Sociolinguistic approaches, rooted in variation theory and diglossia, elucidate how individuals switch between languages and dialects based on social settings and cultural norms. Social identity theory provides a framework for analyzing linguistic hybridity and language ideologies, showcasing how individuals construct and negotiate identities through language use. Real-world case studies illustrate the application of these theories in contexts such as indigenous communities in Amazonia, remote schools in Australia, and digital communication platforms, demonstrating the adaptability of language practices in response to societal structures and technological advancements.

Keywords Sociolinguistic theories · Translanguaging · Language variation · Social identity · Power dynamics · Language ideologies · Linguistic hybridity

Sociolinguistic theories provide a lens through which we can understand the relationship between language, society, and identity. In the context of translanguaging, sociolinguistic perspectives offer valuable insights into

© The Author(s), under exclusive license to Springer Nature   55
Switzerland AG 2024
L. M. Pérez Fernández, *Translanguaging in Multicultural Societies*,
https://doi.org/10.1007/978-3-031-74145-6_5

language variation and multilingualism. This section explores key sociolinguistic approaches, illustrating how societal factors shape the practices of translanguaging among diverse communities.

5.1   Sociolinguistic Approaches to Language Variation and Multilingualism

Sociolinguistic theories emphasize the social aspects of language use, examining how language varies and changes within different social groups. When applied to translanguaging, these approaches help unravel the complexities of multilingual societies. Central to these approaches is the foundational concept of variation theory (Labov, 1972), which contends that language variation is not arbitrary but systematic, intricately intertwined with social, cultural, and contextual factors. In translanguaging practices, this variation becomes evident as individuals fluidly switch between languages and dialects based on social contexts, emphasizing the role of sociocultural influences. Recent scholarship, including Li (2018) and García and Otheguy (2019), has expanded on these ideas, framing translanguaging not just as language mixing, but as a practice that reflects complex social identities and power dynamics. García and Otheguy (2019) argue that translanguaging challenges the traditional notion of languages as separate, stable systems. Instead, they propose the concept of a unitary linguistic repertoire, where multilingual speakers draw from a single, integrated set of linguistic resources. This perspective aligns with Canagarajah's (2011b) view that translanguaging is about how people use their language skills in a flexible and context-aware way, adapting their language choices to fit different social situations and needs.

A significant shift in sociolinguistic thinking, particularly in the works of García (2009b) and Pennycook (2010), has moved the focus from the idea of languages as fixed entities to viewing language as a set of fluid practices that are deeply rooted in local social and cultural activities. This epistemological shift underscores the argument that languages are not discrete, impermeable systems, but are instead mixed, hybrid, and constantly evolving. Pennycook (2010) notably emphasizes that understanding language as a local practice means recognizing that languages and speakers are always in a state of flux, influenced by their specific contexts and interactions.

This approach to language as a practice rather than a static system has led to a clear distinction between the "fixed language approach" and the emerging "fluid languaging approach." The former views languages as stable entities that can be alternated in a planned manner, particularly within educational settings, while the latter sees all communicative practices—including gestures, visual signs, and languages—as part of an integrated, trans-semiotic system. This "fluid languaging approach," as articulated by scholars like Makoni and Pennycook (2007) and Creese and Blackledge (2015), moves beyond the traditional notion of multilingualism to embrace a more dynamic understanding of how people make meaning in complex, rapidly changing environments.

Blommaert's (2014) work on the sociolinguistics of mobility further supports this fluid approach by highlighting how global movement and digital communication have made traditional notions of language and multilingualism insufficient. They argue that traditional terms like "multilingualism" or even "codeswitching" imply separable linguistic units, which do not accurately reflect the interconnected and multimodal ways people communicate today. As a result, scholars now focus on "complex linguistic and semiotic forms" that encompass the full range of resources people use to make meaning in diverse contexts.

At the core of sociolinguistic analysis lie social factors such as age, gender, class, and ethnicity, each leaving an indelible mark on language variation. In translanguaging scenarios, these factors interconnect within the fabric of communication. Generational distinctions emerge, revealing how different age groups within a community employ diverse translanguaging patterns. Consider a multigenerational household where the elders, steeped in regional dialects, serve as linguistic pillars, preserving ancestral languages. Across many cultures, storytelling remains an important means through which historical narratives are transmitted orally across generations, contributing to the preservation of cultural heritage and societal values. Meanwhile, the younger generation, influenced by educational systems and digital platforms, smoothly incorporates English or other global languages into their linguistic repertoire. This linguistic continuum exemplifies the adaptability of language, mirroring the evolving sociocultural setting within families and communities. As García and Li (2014) note, these practices challenge the traditional view of bilingualism as compartmentalized, instead viewing language use as a dynamic and integrated process.

Within multilingual societies, the concept of diglossia emerges as a key sociolinguistic phenomenon. Diglossia refers to the coexistence of two or more language varieties within a community, each assigned specific social functions (Ferguson, 1959). In many postcolonial nations, a diglossic relationship exists between a prestigious, standardized variety (often a colonial language or a national language) and a local, vernacular variety. Translanguaging in diglossic contexts involves a delicate negotiation between these varieties, as individuals transition adeptly between the formal, high-status language and the informal, community-specific vernacular. This interaction highlights the diverse linguistic practices inherent in multilingual societies, providing a comprehensive understanding of their social underpinnings.

In the context of multicultural urban environments, language stands out as a potent marker of social identity. Residents skillfully engage with this linguistic diversity, strategically employing specific languages to convey their social identities. For example, an individual may utilize their ancestral language within their community, reinforcing shared cultural heritage and solidarity. Conversely, when interacting with external entities, they smoothly transition to the dominant national or global language, adjusting their linguistic choices to match prevailing social trends. Consider the case of Chinatown communities in various cities around the world. Within Chinatown neighborhoods, residents often maintain strong ties to their ancestral language, such as Cantonese or Mandarin, using these languages for daily communication within their community to preserve cultural heritage and strengthen solidarity among fellow Chinese residents. Chinatown businesses, social gatherings, and cultural events commonly operate in Chinese languages, nurturing a profound sense of belonging and cultural continuity. On the contrary, when interacting with the broader urban society or engaging in activities outside of Chinatown, residents are proficient in using the dominant local language, such as English. This adaptability allows them to interact effectively with non-Chinese speakers in their everyday lives. These instances showcase the close relationship between language, social identity, and sociocultural contexts, illustrating the diverse ways in which language operates as a powerful social marker.

As García and Li (2014) assert, translanguaging is not merely about using multiple languages but about engaging in complex semiotic practices that transcend traditional language boundaries. This perspective is increasingly recognized as a practical theory of language in the twenty-first century, where communication is inherently multimodal and interconnected, challenging the relevance of viewing languages as fixed and bounded systems.

5.2   Social Identity and Translanguaging: Language, Culture, and Power

Social identity theory (SIT) (Tajfel & Turner, 1979) provides a framework through which we can analyze how language, culture, and power intersect in translanguaging practices. Within the realm of translanguaging, social identity encompasses the various ways individuals perceive themselves in relation to language, culture, and societal structures.

One key aspect of social identity in translanguaging is the notion of linguistic hybridity, which refers to the blending of linguistic elements from multiple languages and dialects, creating a unique and fluid linguistic identity (Sanchez-Stockhammer, 2012). In translanguaging practices, individuals frequently demonstrate linguistic hybridity by integrating vocabulary, grammar, and cultural elements from various languages. In multicultural urban settings, individuals may utilize a hybrid language that incorporates words and expressions from different languages spoken in their community. This linguistic hybridity serves as a marker of their social identity, revealing their multicultural background and interconnected linguistic experiences. For example, across regions such as Asia and Africa, the globalization of English has catalyzed the emergence of hybrid languages like Banglish, Chinglish, and Hinglish, where English integrates with local languages to facilitate communication in diverse contexts (Ahmed & Abu Nayeem, 2023).

Additionally, social identity in translanguaging is closely linked to the concept of language ideologies, which encompass the beliefs, attitudes, and values associated with languages in society (Piller, 2015). These ideologies shape individuals' perceptions of their own languages and the languages of others. In translanguaging practices, language ideologies influence language choices and the negotiation of linguistic identities. For example, in postcolonial societies, colonial languages might be regarded as prestigious, leading individuals to translanguaging practices to gain social recognition and access to opportunities. Alternatively, individuals might resist dominant language ideologies by valorizing their indigenous languages, engaging in translanguaging practices that affirm their cultural heritage and challenge linguistic hierarchies.

Furthermore, social identity in translanguaging is also connected to the power dynamics present in multilingual societies. Language and power are interlinked, with certain languages enjoying social, political, and economic privileges, while others are marginalized. Translanguaging practices, which can challenge or reinforce existing power structures, are particularly evident in educational contexts where teachers' language choices significantly influence students' sense of belonging and academic success. Educators who embrace translanguaging practices create inclusive environments where students can draw upon their full linguistic repertoires, empowering them to express their ideas effectively. Conversely, restrictive language policies in educational institutions may marginalize students who speak non-dominant languages, reinforcing social inequalities.

Moreover, social identity in translanguaging intersects with the already mentioned concept of diglossia, where communities use distinct languages or dialects for different purposes. Translanguaging blurs the boundaries of diglossic languages, allowing individuals to shift between formal and informal linguistic registers based on communicative needs. In this context, individuals might use a formal language variety in academic or professional settings while switching to an informal vernacular in familial or social contexts. This diglossic flexibility in translanguaging reflects the adaptability of social identities, demonstrating how individuals strategically engage with language norms to assert their cultural heritage and social roles.

In summary, social identity in translanguaging is a multifaceted construct shaped by linguistic hybridity, language ideologies, power dynamics, and diglossic practices. Understanding these aspects enriches our comprehension of multilingual interactions, paving the way for inclusive language policies and empowering marginalized communities in their linguistic development.

5.3   Case Studies: Applying Sociolinguistic Theories to Translanguaging Practices

In this section, we present real-world case studies that exemplify the application of sociolinguistic theories to translanguaging practices.

Case Study 1: Linguistic hybridity in the Kotiria community.

The Kotiria people, an indigenous group in the Vaupés region of Amazonia, exhibit a distinctive interplay of language practices, ideologies, and identity construction that challenge traditional notions of monolingual speech. Spanning a territory along the Brazil-Colombia border within the expansive Negro River watershed, the Kotiria number approximately 2,000 individuals. Their societal framework is deeply rooted in a historical and cultural context that emphasizes linguistic diversity and cultural exchange within a framework of patrilineal descent and exogamic marriage practices (Stenzel & Khoo, 2016). Throughout centuries of interaction with neighboring groups such as the Baniwa, Tariana, Desano, Tukano, and Kubeo, the Kotiria have developed a distinctive multilingual regional system described by Sorensen (1967) as "a large, culturally homogeneous area where multilingualism—and polylingualism in the individual—is the cultural norm" (p. 671). Stenzel and Khoo (2016) explore linguistic hybridity through the case of Eliana, who lives in the Kotiria village of Poraque Ponta. She fluently speaks her father's language, Kotiria, which serves as the primary public language in her village and at the Kotiria Indigenous School located in Carurú Cachoeira. Eliana also maintains proficiency in her mother's language, Tukano, which is widely spoken among the in-marrying wives in Poraque Ponta. Additionally, she has acquired competence in Portuguese, largely through her educational experience at the Kotiria Indigenous School. Established in 2002 and expanded to include high school education in 2006, this school initially used Portuguese as the language of instruction, reflecting its role as the national language and necessary for communication outside indigenous contexts.

Despite efforts to incorporate Kotiria language into the curriculum, Portuguese remains dominant due to ongoing educational developments and societal expectations (Stenzel & Khoo, 2016). Eliana's linguistic repertoire reflects this blend of languages, each serving specific functions within her community and beyond.

A central event in Eliana's community life is the graduation ceremony, a vibrant amalgamation of indigenous traditions and adapted non-indigenous elements. The ceremony spans two days and involves meticulous preparations, including traditional rituals like applying skin paint and attending a mass in the village chapel. Graduates, including Eliana, present their monographs—academic papers typically written in Portuguese but orally presented in Kotiria—to celebrate their achievements and showcase their knowledge of Kotiria history, culture, or traditional practices (Stenzel & Khoo, 2016).

Eliana's narrative exemplifies fluid language use where she naturally transitions between Kotiria, Portuguese, and Tukano languages. For example, she integrates Portuguese lexical items such as *formatura* (graduation) and *monografia* (monograph) into her Kotiria discourse. These borrowings are not isolated instances of code-switching but are integrated into Kotiria grammatical structures and marked with appropriate morphological elements, demonstrating a harmonious fusion of linguistic resources (Stenzel & Khoo, 2016). This serves pragmatic functions, filling lexical gaps and conveying precise meanings that reflect both indigenous and non-indigenous cultural influences.

Eliana's discourse appears to challenge regional norms regarding appropriate language use and contradicts prevalent beliefs that discourage language mixing, which are often perceived as jeopardizing social cohesion.

Case Study 2: Translanguaging in remote indigenous schools in Australia.

Educational institutions serve as crucial arenas where sociolinguistic theories intersect with translanguaging practices. Indigenous children in remote areas of Australia, such as northern Queensland, the Northern Territory, and Western Australia, are often born into diverse and multilingual language contexts (Wigglesworth, 2020). These linguistic environments involve both Traditional Indigenous Languages (TILs) and various creole languages, which significantly influence the children's educational experiences. Indigenous children in these remote regions may speak a TIL, a variety of Kriol, or a combination of both.

When Indigenous children enter formal schooling, they encounter English—often for the first time in a structured setting. This is in stark contrast to children in urban areas who are more likely to be exposed to English at home or in their communities. For many Indigenous children, the transition to an English-dominant school system is akin to learning a foreign language, given the limited exposure to English in their early years (Simpson & Wigglesworth, 2018) and the little to no integration of the children's first languages. This lack of linguistic recognition extends to creole languages, which are not seen as valid educational tools. As a result, children's linguistic repertoires are undervalued, hindering their potential for academic success (Wigglesworth, 2020).

In this context, translanguaging offers a promising approach to integrating Indigenous languages into educational settings, focusing on the process of achieving effective communication rather than merely switching between languages. As Wigglesworth (2020) points out, although teachers cannot realistically be expected to learn all the languages spoken by their students, they should recognize and value the students' linguistic abilities. In remote areas of Australia where Indigenous languages are still spoken, most classrooms are supported by Indigenous Teaching Assistants proficient in both English and the children's native languages and whose presence is instrumental in facilitating this recognition and support within the classroom.

Case Study 3: Translanguaging in digital communication.

The digital realm offers a unique space for exploring translanguaging practices influenced by sociolinguistic factors. Social media platforms, online forums, and digital communities facilitate multilingual interactions, enabling individuals to express their identities in diverse linguistic forms. Sociolinguistic analyses of online discourse reveal the impact of social networks, cultural affiliations, and digital language ideologies on translanguaging practices. Users strategically switch between languages, employing specific linguistic features to convey social solidarity, humor, or cultural pride. For instance, in online diaspora communities, individuals use translanguaging to maintain connections with their homeland, reinforcing shared cultural norms and linguistic traditions. The study of these digital interactions through sociolinguistic lenses offers scholars insights into the evolving nature of translanguaging in the digital age, emphasizing the importance of understanding sociocultural contexts in online multilingual communication.

The advent of digital communication technologies, particularly smartphones, has revolutionized how individuals bridge linguistic divides, especially in contexts of resettlement and migration. McCaffrey and Taha (2019) discuss how Middle Eastern refugee families in northern New Jersey harness these ubiquitous devices to overcome initial language barriers during resettlement. Such devices, equipped with apps like WhatsApp, Google Maps, and various social media platforms, not only facilitate daily tasks but also foster multimodal forms of communication across languages and cultures (Madianou, 2014).

Smartphones played a central role in helping resettled refugees move around their new environment, especially in metropolitan areas like New York. As families became more integrated into community activities and acquired vehicles, smartphones with GPS capabilities became essential tools for navigating unfamiliar streets and locations. This was particularly significant for men who secured jobs as Uber and Lyft drivers (McCaffrey & Taha, 2019), where basic English proficiency combined with GPS navigation enabled them to operate efficiently across diverse geographical landscapes.

Mobile translation apps such as Google Translate and Microsoft Translator were indispensable for overcoming language barriers in various everyday situations. Participants used these apps during medical appointments, visits to welfare offices, and interactions at parent-teacher conferences. However, the effectiveness of MT apps was often compromised by challenges such as difficulties in translating colloquial expressions, idiomatic phrases, and nuanced cultural meanings. As a result, family members frequently collaborated to ensure accurate communication, highlighting the resilience and adaptability of refugee communities in managing these technological limitations. Despite these challenges, younger participants, particularly school-aged children, embraced MT apps enthusiastically not only for translation but also for social interactions and learning in ESL (English as a Second Language) classes, where these tools facilitated peer communication and knowledge exchange in multiple languages.

In summary, smartphones and mobile translation apps emerged as fundamental tools for resettled refugees, bridging linguistic gaps and supporting both daily activities and broader integration efforts.

These case studies illustrate the intricate relationship between sociolinguistic theories and translanguaging practices in diverse contexts. The application of sociolinguistic frameworks enables researchers, educators, and policymakers to unravel the nature of multilingual interactions, promoting inclusive language policies and empowering communities to preserve their linguistic heritage. Through sociolinguistic analyses of real-life situations, we enhance our understanding of translanguaging as a dynamic sociocultural phenomenon, enriching both academic discourse and practical applications in multilingual societies.

References

Ahmed, F., & Abu Nayeem, M. (2023). Linguistic hybridity and cultural preservation: A qualitative exploration of cultural identity. *Journal of English Studies*, *1*(1), 85–99.

Blommaert, J. (2014). From mobility to complexity in sociolinguistic theory and method. In N. Coupland (Ed.), *Sociolinguistics: Theoretical Debates* (pp. 242–259). Cambridge University Press.

Canagarajah, S. (2011b). Codemeshing in academic writing: Identifying teachable strategies of translanguaging. *The Modern Language Journal*, *95*(3), 401–417. https://doi.org/10.1111/j.1540-4781.2011.01207.x

Creese, A., & Blackledge, A. (2015). Translanguaging and identity in educational settings. *Annual Review of Applied Linguistics*, *35*, 20–35. https://doi.org/10.1017/S0267190514000233

Ferguson, C. A. (1959). *Diglossia. Word*, *15*(2), 325–340. https://doi.org/10.1080/00437956.1959.11659702

García, O., & Li, W. (2014). *Translanguaging: Language, bilingualism and education*. Palgrave Macmillan.

García, O. (2009a). *Bilingual education in the 21st century: A global perspective*. Wiley-Blackwell.

García, O. (2009b). Education, multilingualism and translanguaging in the 21st century. In T. Skutnabb-Kangas, R. Phillipson, A. Mohanty, & M. Panda (Ed.), *Social justice through multilingual education* (pp. 140–158). Multilingual Matters. https://doi.org/10.21832/9781847691910-011

García, O., & Otheguy, R. (2019). Plurilingualism and translanguaging: Commonalities and divergences. *International Journal of Bilingual Education and Bilingualism*, *23*(1), 17–35. https://doi.org/10.1080/13670050.2019.1598932

Labov, William. (1972). *Sociolinguistic patterns*. University of Pennsylvania Press.

Li, W. (2018). Translanguaging as a practical theory of language. *Applied Linguistics*, *1*, 9–30. https://doi.org/10.1093/applin/amx039

Madianou, M. (2014). Polymedia communication and Mediatized migration. In K. Lundby (Ed.), *Mediatization of communication* (pp. 323–348). De Gruyter.

Makoni, S., & Pennycook, A. (2007). *Disinventing and reconstituting languages*. Multilingual Matters.

McCaffrey, K. T., & Taha, M. C. (2019). Rethinking the digital divide: Smartphones as translanguaging tools among Middle Eastern Refugees in New Jersey. *Annals of Anthropological Practice*, *43*(2), 26–38. https://doi.org/10.1111/napa.12126

Pennycook, A. (2010). *Language as a local practice*. Routledge.

Piller, I. (2015). Language ideologies. In K. Tracy, C. Ilie, & T. Sandel (Eds.), *The International encyclopedia of language and social interaction* (Vol.

2, pp. 917–927). (The Wiley Blackwell-ICA international encyclopedias of communication). Wiley-Blackwell.

Sanchez-Stockhammer, C. (2012). Hybridization in language. In P. W. Stockhammer (Ed.), *Conceptualizing cultural hybridization: A transdisciplinary approach* (pp. 133–157). Springer. https://doi.org/10.1007/978-3-642-218 46-0_9

Simpson, J., & Wigglesworth, G. (2018). Language diversity in Indigenous Australia in the 21st century. *Current Issues in Language Planning, 20*(1), 67–80. https://doi.org/10.1080/14664208.2018.1503389

Sorensen, A. (1967). Multilingualism in the Northwest Amazon. *American Anthropologist, 69,* 670–684.

Stenzel, K., & Khoo, V. (2016). Linguistic hybridity: A case study in the Kotiria community. *Critical Multilingualism Studies, 4*(2), 75–110.

Tajfel, H., & Turner, J. C. (1979). An integrative theory of inter-group conflict. In W. G. Austin & S. Worchel (Eds.), *The social psychology of inter-group relations* (pp. 33–47). Brooks/Cole.

Wigglesworth, G. (2020). Remote indigenous education and translanguaging. *TESOL in Context, 29*(1), 95–113.

CHAPTER 6

Cognitive Approaches to Translanguaging

Abstract This chapter explores cognitive approaches to translanguaging, focusing on metacognition and cognitive flexibility as key concepts. It examines how bilingual individuals employ these cognitive processes to manage and optimize their language use in various contexts. The chapter addresses the role of metacognition in monitoring and evaluating language choices, enhancing communicative strategies and learning outcomes. Additionally, it investigates cognitive flexibility as a mechanism for seamlessly shifting between languages to meet communicative demands, thereby fostering linguistic proficiency and effective multilingual communication.

Keywords Cognitive approaches · Translanguaging · Metacognition · Cognitive flexibility · Bilingualism

The inherent nature of language choices within translanguaging aligns with cognitive approaches, highlighting how cognitive processes naturally adapt to meet linguistic demands. This adaptability unfolds across various cognitive dimensions, notably metacognition, cognitive flexibility, or neurocognitive foundations.

L. M. Pérez Fernández, *Translanguaging in Multicultural Societies*, https://doi.org/10.1007/978-3-031-74145-6_6

67

6.1   The Intersection Between Translanguaging and Metacognition

Metacognition, the ability to evaluate one's own cognitive performance (Flavell, 1979), is paramount in translanguaging. In educational settings, bilingual learners often demonstrate advanced metacognitive skills. They possess a deep awareness of their language repertoires, understanding when and how to draw from different languages to enhance their learning experiences. For instance, a bilingual student engaged in a CLIL history lesson might incorporate historical terms from both their native language and the language of instruction, leading to an insightful understanding of historical events. This metacognitive engagement exemplifies the cognitive depth inherent in translanguaging, demonstrating how multilingual individuals strategically use their linguistic resources to enrich their cognitive processes.

At the core of metacognition lies strategic decision-making, a cognitive process deeply intertwined with translanguaging. Individuals proficient in multiple languages thoughtfully manage the linguistic setting, deciding when to employ code-switching or draw from their language repertoire. This metacognitive approach involves evaluating the communicative demands of a situation and making intentional choices to optimize language use for effective expression. Such decision-making extends beyond the immediate context, laying the groundwork for a post-communication reflective process. Individuals evaluate the effectiveness of their language choices, considering alternative strategies for future interactions. This reflective practice enhances metacognitive skills, encouraging an ongoing engagement that leads individuals to critically assess the success of their communicative efforts. Therefore, continual metacognitive involvement serves as a foundation for adjusting and refining language use in subsequent interactions.

Furthermore, translanguaging becomes instrumental in problem-solving scenarios, where metacognitive strategies come to the forefront. In a foreign language classroom, imagine a Spanish student dealing with a challenging English language exercise. Faced with a complex passage, the student, employing metacognitive strategies, strategically taps into their native language. Through the application of translanguaging, the learner effectively manages unfamiliar vocabulary and sentence structures, transforming their native Spanish into a problem-solving tool. This intentional use of translanguaging demonstrates the student's metacognitive agility and underscores the valuable role it plays in overcoming linguistic challenges within the context of language learning.

Metacognition within translanguaging extends beyond individual strategic decision-making and reflective practices. It encompasses collaborative metacognition, where learners engage in shared cognitive processes to enhance understanding (Goos et al., 2002). In a multilingual classroom setting, students may collaboratively employ translanguaging during group discussions or projects, negotiating language choices collectively to ensure effective communication and shared comprehension. This shared reflective process contributes to both individual metacognitive growth and the development of a collective metacognitive community within the learning environment.

Another dimension of metacognition in translanguaging involves the concept of "cognitive bridging," a term which refers to the mental connection between an abstract goal and the specific action to achieve it, or the logical connection between how we do something and why we do it (Katz & Byrne, 2018). Translanguaging serves as a cognitive bridge, facilitating the transfer of knowledge and concepts between languages. In content-based language learning, such as a science class where Spanish-speaking students are introduced to the details of cellular biology in English, translanguaging serves as a tool to bridge their existing knowledge in their native language with the new concepts presented in the foreign language. This cognitive bridging enhances metacognitive connections between linguistic repertoires, leading to a deeper understanding of subject matter and promoting effective learning strategies across languages. For instance, when facing cellular biology terms such as "cell membrane" or "mitochondria," students may engage in discussions using a blend of Spanish and English. They describe the functions of these cellular components in Spanish, drawing parallels to their existing knowledge, and then smoothly transition to using the English terms within the lesson context. The intentional use of translanguaging as a cognitive bridge exemplifies metacognitive adaptability and the strategic application of language resources to optimize learning outcomes. Learners discuss the cell's structure using Spanish terminology, connecting it to their prior knowledge, and subsequently introduce the English equivalents to strengthen their grasp of scientific concepts. In this manner, translanguaging functions as a cognitive bridge, facilitating a more straightforward transition between languages and empowering students to address the challenges of scientific language while enhancing their metacognitive connections between linguistic resources. The result is a more comprehensive understanding of the subject matter and the development of effective learning strategies across both Spanish and English.

6.2   Cognitive Flexibility in Translanguaging

Translanguaging demonstrates how language use adapts fluidly to meet immediate communicative needs. At the forefront of this adaptability is cognitive flexibility (Bialystok & Senman, 2004), the capacity to shift between different cognitive processes or adapt to changing mental demands.

Bilingual individuals, by nature, exhibit enhanced cognitive flexibility as they constantly move between two linguistic systems, adapting to contextual demands. For instance, a bilingual professional negotiating business deals might change from using their native language for informal discussions to employing a second language for formal negotiations. This fluidity underscores their language proficiency and highlights the cognitive agility essential for effective translanguaging practices.

One notable dimension of cognitive flexibility in translanguaging is observed when students smoothly switch between their native language and target language to express ideas. For instance, during a classroom discussion on a complex topic, a Spanish student might articulate a thought in Spanish, showcasing a profound understanding of the concept. Recognizing the need to communicate effectively in an English-speaking environment, the student adeptly transitions to expressing the same idea in English. This cognitive flexibility allows learners to adapt their language use to different contexts, refining their ability to shift between languages in response to communicative demands.

Cognitive flexibility becomes particularly valuable when learners encounter gaps in vocabulary during foreign language acquisition. Translanguaging emerges as a strategic tool, offering learners a deliberate pathway to leverage their native language as a bridge, thereby improving both comprehension and expression. In the context of a CLIL geography lesson, students might employ their native language to understand unfamiliar terms before integrating them into their responses in the target language. This approach facilitates a deeper understanding of the subject matter and emphasizes the cognitive flexibility indispensable for effectively overcoming the varied linguistic challenges encountered within the learning environment.

Moreover, cognitive flexibility extends beyond linguistic adjustments and encompasses a broader spectrum of cognitive functions. It involves the capacity to embrace varying perspectives, consider alternative meanings, and modify communication strategies in response to evolving communicative contexts. The translanguaging experience, therefore, becomes a manifestation of the relationship between cognitive flexibility and linguistic adaptability.

6.3 Case Study: Translanguaging and Cognitive Approaches in L2 Listening and Writing Skills

The following case study (Robillos, 2023) explores how translanguaging aligns with cognitive approaches, particularly in enhancing metacognitive strategy use in L2 learning. The study focuses on a group of 16 first-year college students enrolled in a TESOL program in Northeastern Thailand. These students, who were simultaneous Thai-Isarn bilinguals, participated in an intervention designed to improve their listening comprehension and writing skills in English through the strategic use of translanguaging.

In this educational setting, English was the medium of instruction for nearly all subjects, yet many students struggled with listening comprehension in English due to the traditional methods of teaching that focused on testing rather than skill development. The strict English-only policy of the program further compounded these difficulties. To address these challenges, the instructor implemented a metacognitive approach to listening and writing tasks, integrating translanguaging as a core component. Over 11 sessions, the intervention allowed students to use their entire linguistic repertoire (Thai, Isarn, and English) during metacognitive stages of planning, monitoring, and evaluation in listening comprehension tasks. Students were encouraged to translanguage during group discussions to deepen their understanding and to enhance their ability to process and articulate their thoughts in English.

The qualitative results provided key insights into how translanguaging supported the students' learning process. During the planning stage, students used their L1 to discuss their background knowledge and expectations about the listening tasks. For example, one participant noted that being able to discuss the content in L1 before tackling the listening task in English helped them feel more prepared and confident: "Translanguaging allows us to engage in meaningful conversations and eases the process of clarifying and negotiating ideas. Solely depending on English as the language of thought can be quite challenging" (Robillos, 2023, p. 119). This ability to access their full linguistic repertoire in L1 allowed students to bridge the gap between prior knowledge and new information, facilitating a deeper cognitive engagement with the task.

The monitoring phase also highlighted the value of translanguaging, as participants used their L1 to collaborate and solve listening comprehension problems. One student shared how discussing ideas in their L1 helped them articulate their thoughts more fluently: "Because we don't hesitate to convey our thoughts in English and use Thai, Isarn, Lanna, it has enabled us to engage in discussions more naturally and fluently" (Robillos, 2023, p. 119). This fluid switching between languages allowed participants to compare their understanding of the listening selections with their peers, resolve discrepancies, and improve their comprehension of the content.

In the evaluation stage, students reflected on their listening performance and identified areas for improvement, again using translanguaging to communicate complex ideas. For instance, one participant explained that using their L1 during group evaluations allowed them to better understand the feedback and corrections on their writing tasks: "Using Thai or Isarn language during the sharing activity made me acutely aware of my L1, including Thai idioms and complex expressions that are challenging to directly translate into L2" (Robillos, 2023, p. 120). This reflection and evaluation in L1 helped students pinpoint grammatical and structural errors in their L2 writing, leading to improvements in subsequent tasks.

The quantitative results supported these qualitative findings, showing significant improvements in the participants' listening comprehension and writing abilities. The average post-test score increased from 9.19 to 15.56, and there was a clear upward trend in the students' quiz results over time. The grammar and structure component showed the most improvement, which aligns with the qualitative feedback that translanguaging facilitated deeper discussions on these areas. Students were able to identify and correct errors more effectively when they discussed them in their L1 during group activities (Robillos, 2023).

Participants also expressed overwhelmingly positive perceptions of translanguaging, viewing it not as a hindrance but as a tool that supported their L2 learning. One participant emphasized that translanguaging helped them engage more critically with the content: "The use of translanguaging in collaborative monitoring activities deepened our comprehension of the topic's context and boosted our proficiency in applying listening strategies" (Robillos, 2023, p. 120). This perception underscores the cognitive benefits of using L1 strategically in the learning process, particularly in tasks that require deep understanding and critical thinking.

In conclusion, the integration of translanguaging within a cognitive framework, particularly through metacognitive strategy use, proves to be an effective pedagogical approach in L2 education. This case study demonstrates that when students are allowed to draw on their entire linguistic repertoire, they can achieve significant cognitive and academic gains.

REFERENCES

Bialystok, E., & Senman, L. (2004). Executive processes in appearance-reality tasks: The role of inhibition of attention and symbolic representation. *Child Development*, *75*, 562–579. https://doi.org/10.1111/j.1467-8624. 2004.00693.x

Flavell, J. H. (1979). Metacognition and cognitive monitoring: A new area of cognitive–developmental inquiry. *American Psychologist*, *34*(10), 906–911. https://doi.org/10.1037/0003-066X.34.10.906

Goos, M., Galbraith, P., & Renshaw, P. (2002). Socially mediated metacognition: Creating collaborative zones of proximal development in small group problem solving. *Educational Studies in Mathematics*, *49*, 193–223. https://doi.org/10.1023/A:1016209010120

Katz, S. J., & Byrne, S. (2018). Cognitive bridging: Using strategic communication to connect abstract goals with the means to achieve them. *Health Communication*, *34*(4), 484–499. https://doi.org/10.1080/104 10236.2018.1428848

Robillos R. J. (2023). Exploring Translanguaging during metacognitive strategy use on L2 listening and writing skills. *Journal of Language and Education*, *9*(3), 110–128. https://doi.org/10.17323/jle.2023.14329

CHAPTER 7

Psycholinguistic Perspectives

Abstract This chapter delves into psycholinguistic perspectives on translanguaging, exploring the relationship between cognitive processes and language use. It examines how translanguaging draws upon psycholinguistic theories to elucidate its mechanisms and implications, highlighting concepts such as multicompetence and language transfer within bilingual contexts. The chapter also investigates the cognitive aspects of language processing in bilingual individuals, shedding light on how different languages interact in the mind. Furthermore, it explores the intersection of translanguaging with social-emotional learning, emphasizing its role in fostering emotional well-being, identity development, and inclusive educational environments. Through these lenses, the chapter offers insights into how psycholinguistic frameworks enrich our understanding of translanguaging practices across diverse linguistic and cultural settings.

Keywords Psycholinguistics · Translanguaging · Cognitive processes · Language transfer · Bilingualism · Social-emotional learning · Language processing

Psycholinguistics combines psychology and linguistics, merging the investigation of mind and behavior with the study of language. Essentially, it can be defined as the exploration of the relationship between the human mind and language, delving into the cognitive processes within the brain during language production and perception. This field is concerned with understanding how the mind interacts with language, unraveling the relationship between cognition and linguistic processes.

7.1 Psycholinguistic Aspects of Translanguaging

The term "translanguaging" is deeply connected to psycholinguistics, drawing upon the theoretical frameworks and concepts within this field to elucidate its nature and implications. Initially, the term itself is a composite of "trans-" and "languaging," with the notion of "languaging" originating from psycholinguistics (Dumrukcic, 2022). Scholars like Myachykov et al. (2013) and Spiridonov & Ezrina (2016) have examined how language use relates to consciousness and cognitive processes, emphasizing the integration of multiple languages in a cohesive system.

Cook's (2016) concept of "multicompetence" further enriches our understanding of translanguaging. "Multicompetence refers to the overall system of a mind or a community that uses more than one language" (Cook, 2016, p. 3). This perspective shifts the focus from viewing languages as separate, isolated systems to understanding them as interconnected within a single cognitive framework. In the context of translanguaging, this integrated view of multilingual competence aligns well with the practice of drawing from a cohesive linguistic repertoire rather than compartmentalizing languages.

Grosjean (1989) supports this integrated view by arguing that bilinguals have a unique, holistic linguistic configuration that reflects the coexistence and constant interaction of multiple languages. This aligns with the core concept of translanguaging, where bilinguals draw from their entire linguistic repertoire, transcending the traditional labels of L1 and L2.

Translanguaging's connection to psycholinguistics becomes particularly evident in examining the cognitive aspects of language processing in bilinguals. Findings from behavioral and neurolinguistic studies indicate an overlap of various languages in the bilingual brain, with different labels for the same concept. The idea of different language modes within the linguistic repertoire, activated based on circumstances, resonates with the psycholinguistic understanding of language processing.

In the exploration of psycholinguistic interactions within bilingual or multilingual environments, another fundamental aspect to scrutinize is language transfer—the phenomenon where language learners apply elements from their native language to the target language. Theoretical frameworks, such as the Interlanguage Hypothesis (Selinker, 1972) and the Linguistic Proximity Model (Odlin, 1989), provide a conceptual foundation for interpreting how language transfer manifests in multilingual environments.

On the one hand, the Interlanguage Hypothesis, proposed by Selinker (1972), posits that language learners undergo an evolving intermediate stage in the process of acquiring a second language, termed "interlanguage." This stage represents a system with unique rules and structures that learners construct as they progress toward full language proficiency. In the context of language transfer, the Interlanguage Hypothesis suggests that learners may exhibit features of their native language in their evolving interlanguage, shedding light on how language transfer unfolds during the multilingual learning process. This aligns with the translanguaging paradigm, emphasizing the flexible use of multiple languages. The evolving interlanguage, as proposed by Selinker, resonates with the fluidity inherent in translanguaging practices, where learners move through a linguistic environment with permeable boundaries between languages.

On the other hand, the Linguistic Proximity Model (Odlin, 1989) focuses on the linguistic similarities and differences between the native and target languages. It suggests that the extent of linguistic proximity between the two languages influences the likelihood and nature of language transfer. The model emphasizes factors such as structural similarities and lexical overlap as crucial determinants. Odlin's Linguistic Proximity Model acknowledges that not all aspects of a language are equally transferable and highlights the importance of considering linguistic proximity in understanding transfer patterns. In the context of translanguaging, this model finds resonance, as translanguaging acknowledges the strategic selection of linguistic resources based on contextual appropriateness and linguistic proximity. Both frameworks contribute insights into how language transfer operates, aligning with the translanguaging paradigm's emphasis on the flexible use of multiple languages in multilingual settings.

7.2   Social Emotional
Learning in Translanguaging

In recent years, the intersection of translanguaging and social-emotional learning (SEL) (Kim et al., 2022) has emerged as a significant area in educational research, recognizing the significance of students' emotional well-being and its connection to their language development and academic success.

Translanguaging, when observed in diverse contexts, proves to be a powerful tool that taps into individuals' reservoirs of knowledge, creating what can be described as a third space—a realm where authentic expression of multicultural resources and identities is nurtured. Aligned with SEL principles, this practice actively supports the development of linguistic skills while promoting self-awareness, social acuity, and the ability to build relationships (Song et al., 2022). This approach also contributes to cultivating a socially just and inclusive environment, acknowledging and leveraging diverse knowledge and experiences that may otherwise remain unseen in traditional educational settings.

The positive emotions generated by individuals engaged in translanguaging extend beyond academic settings, enhancing adaptability to new environments and creating a conducive atmosphere for learning. In viewing translanguaging through the lens of SEL strategy, its role in providing emotional and social support to multilingual individuals becomes evident. Acting as a scaffold for emotions, particularly amid the anxiety associated with engaging with unfamiliar linguistic contexts, translanguaging becomes a facilitator for increased participation in various tasks, positively influencing learners' motivation to communicate (Back et al., 2020). This resonates with Krashen's (1982) concept of an affective filter, where reduced anxiety is crucial for effective language acquisition.

The perspective of bilingual teachers adds depth to the understanding of how translanguaging supports multilingual learners emotionally. Valuing linguistic and cultural backgrounds through translanguaging nurtures pride and a sense of belonging, which helps reduce feelings of isolation and anxiety (Tsokalidou & Skourtou, 2020). Beyond the classroom, translanguaging, as explored by Dovchin (2021), transforms into a safe emotional space for ESL immigrants, assisting them in managing and expressing the emotional and psychological difficulties stemming from adverse life experiences (Piller & Takahashi, 2011).

Addressing the psychological challenges faced by international students, as highlighted by Dovchin (2020), underscores the severe consequences of linguistic racism. Translanguaging becomes a crucial means for students to cope with emotional and psychological difficulties, offering a supportive environment for managing linguistic challenges and cultural adaptation.

7.3 Case Study: Bilingual Lexical Processing in L1 and L2 Using Eye-Tracking

Tham et al. (2019) investigated how bilinguals process lexical cues in their first language (L1) and second language (L2) through an eye-tracking methodology. This exploration is highly relevant to psycholinguistics, a field which focuses on how individuals perceive and produce language, how language is represented in the mind, and how bilinguals manage multiple languages simultaneously.

The study was conducted with 31 Malaysian bilingual undergraduates, aged around 21, all of whom were proficient in Malay (L1) and English (L2). The participants were second-year students majoring in English Language Studies or Linguistics at a Malaysian public university. The participants were tested using eye-tracking technology to understand how they process novel words accompanied by either L1 or L2 cues. Importantly, these bilinguals had been exposed to both languages from an early age, and the study's design taps into how they engaged with both languages during a reading task.

The study utilized an eye-tracker, a device that records eye movements to measure how long participants fixate on specific words and cues during a reading task. Eye-tracking is particularly useful for psycholinguistic research because it provides precise, real-time data on cognitive processing without relying on participants' subjective responses. This allowed the researchers to observe bilinguals' cognitive load when processing novel words in English (L2) with accompanying cues either in their first language (Malay) or in their second language (English).

Participants were given short paragraphs with novel words—words unfamiliar to them. These novel words were followed by lexical cues either in L1 or in L2. For example, in one sentence, a novel word like "staveners" might appear with the L1 cue "pendengar" (meaning "listener" in Malay), while in another sentence, the same word might appear with an L2 cue. The participants' fixation times were recorded to determine whether they processed L1 and L2 cues differently when encountering novel words.

One of the key findings was that the fixation times on novel words were similar regardless of whether the cues were in L1 or L2. The participants spent a comparable amount of time processing words accompanied by cues in both languages. This result aligns with psycholinguistic theories like the Bilingual Interactive Activation Plus (BIA +) model (Dijkstra & van Heuven, 2002), which suggests that bilinguals simultaneously activate both languages when processing linguistic information, even if they are reading in one language. The bilingual mind does not rigidly compartmentalize languages; instead, both linguistic systems are active during reading and comprehension. For instance, participants showed no significant difference in the time they spent fixating on novel words, regardless of whether the lexical cues were presented in Malay or English. This finding supports the psycholinguistic view that bilinguals manage both languages dynamically, drawing on their full linguistic repertoire when interpreting novel words.

The study also examined the acquisition of new vocabulary through incidental learning. The participants completed a post-test to assess how many of the novel words they had learned during the reading task. Similar to the fixation time results, the test scores revealed no significant difference in vocabulary acquisition between words accompanied by L1 cues and those with L2 cues. This finding suggests that bilinguals can learn new words equally well regardless of whether the contextual support comes from their first or second language. This reinforces the idea that bilinguals use both languages flexibly and interchangeably when learning new vocabulary. The use of L1 does not impede the acquisition of L2 and vice versa. This aligns with research suggesting that bilinguals' cognitive processing is highly adaptable, allowing them to draw on their knowledge of both languages to support comprehension and learning (Dijkstra & van Heuven, 2002).

During post-test interviews, participants often reported that they felt they spent more time and cognitive effort on L1 cues, even though the eye-tracking data did not support this perception. The discrepancy between participants' subjective experiences and their actual eye movements highlights a key psycholinguistic insight: much of language processing occurs below the level of conscious awareness. Bilinguals might not always be aware of the extent to which they rely on both languages during cognitive tasks, suggesting that translanguaging is an intuitive, subconscious strategy for managing linguistic input. This insight is crucial from a psycholinguistic standpoint because it reveals the complex cognitive mechanisms bilinguals use in real-time language processing. Despite participants' preferences for L1 or L2, their cognitive processing, as measured by eye-tracking, was equally efficient across both languages, further supporting the notion of non-selective access in bilingual lexical processing (Marian & Spivey, 2003).

In conclusion, this study demonstrates how translanguaging aligns with psycholinguistic theories, showing that bilinguals draw on both their L1 and L2 when processing new vocabulary. The fluid use of multiple languages in cognitive tasks, as observed in the similar fixation times and vocabulary acquisition results, supports the psycholinguistic understanding that bilinguals activate both language systems simultaneously.

References

Back, M., Han, M., & Weng, S.-C. A. (2020). Emotional scaffolding for emergent multilingual learners through translanguaging: Case stories. *Language and Education, 34*(1), 1–20. https://doi.org/10.1080/09500782.2020.1744638

Cook, V. (2016). Premises of multi-competence. In V. Cook & W. Li (Eds.), *The Cambridge handbook of linguistic multicompetence* (pp. 1–25). Cambridge University Press.

Dovchin S. (2020). The psychological damages of linguistic racism and international students in Australia. *International Journal of Bilingual Education and Bilingualism, 23*(7), 804–818. https://doi.org/10.1080/13670050.2020.1759504

Dovchin, S. (2021). Translanguaging, emotionality, and English as a second language immigrants: Mongolian background women in Australia. *TESOL Quarterly, 55*(3), 839–865.

Dijkstra, T., & van Heuven, W. J. B. (2002). The architecture of the bilingual visual word recognition system: From identification to decision. *Bilingualism: Language and Cognition, 5*(3), 175–197.

Dumrukcic, N. (2022). *Translanguaging and the bilingual brain*. De Gruyter.

Grosjean, F. (1989). Neurolinguists, beware! The bilingual is not two monolinguals in one person. *Brain and Language, 36*(1), 3–15. https://doi.org/10.1016/0093-934x(89)90048-5

Kim, D., Lim, J. H., & An, J. (2022). The quality and effectiveness of Social-Emotional Learning (SEL) intervention studies in Korea: A meta-analysis. *PLoS ONE, 17*(6), 1–18. https://doi.org/10.1371/journal.pone.0269996

Krashen, S. D. (1982). *Principles and practice in second language acquisition.* Pergamon Press Inc.

Marian, V., & Spivey, M. (2003). Bilingual and monolingual processing of competing lexical items. *Applied Psycholinguistics, 24*(2), 173–193. https://doi.org/10.1017/S0142716403000092

Myachykov, A., Scheepers, C., & Shtyrov, Y. (2013). Interfaces between language and cognition. *Frontiers in Psychology, 4*(258). https://doi.org/10.3389/fpsyg.2013.00258

Odlin, T. (1989). *Language transfer. Cross-linguistic influence in language learning.* Cambridge University Press.

Piller, I., & Takahashi, K. (2011). Language, migration and human rights. In R. Wodak, B. Johnstone, & P. Kerswill (Eds.), *The SAGE Handbook of Sociolinguistics* (583–597). SAGE Publications. https://doi.org/10.4135/9781446200957.

Selinker, L. (1972). Interlanguage. *International Review of Applied Linguistics, 10*, 209–231.

Song, J., Howard, D., & Olazabal-Arias, W. (2022). Translanguaging as a strategy for supporting multilingual learners' social emotional learning. *Education Sciences, 12*(7), 475. https://doi.org/10.3390/educsci12070475

Spiridonov, V., & Ezrina, E. (2016). The interaction of several languages in the cognitive system. *SSRN Electronic Journal, 2*(4), 12–29. https://doi.org/10.2139/ssrn.2664523

Tham, I., Chau, M. H., & Thang, S. M. (2019). Bilinguals' processing of lexical cues in L1 and L2: An eye-tracking study. *Computer Assisted Language Learning, 33*(7), 665–687. https://doi.org/10.1080/09588221.2019.1588329

Tsokalidou, R., & Skourtou, E. (2020). Translanguaging as a culturally sustaining pedagogical approach: Bi/Multilingual educators' perspectives. In J. A. Panagiotopoulou, L. Rosen, & J. Strzykala (Eds.), *Inclusion, education and translanguaging* (pp. 219–235). Springer. https://doi.org/10.1007/978-3-658-28128-1_1

CHAPTER 8

Sociocultural Perspectives

Abstract This chapter explores sociocultural perspectives on translanguaging, emphasizing the dynamic interplay between language practices and social contexts. It investigates how translanguaging aligns with sociocultural theories, particularly through concepts like the Zone of Proximal Development (ZPD) and cultural mediation, highlighting its role in collaborative learning and identity construction. The chapter delves into the notion of cultural repertoires, showcasing how translanguaging integrates diverse linguistic resources to enrich communication and reinforce cultural identities within communities. Moreover, it examines the influence of sociolinguistic norms and language ideologies on translanguaging behaviors, illustrating how individuals express cultural meanings through their linguistic choices.

Keywords Sociocultural theories · Translanguaging · Zone of Proximal Development (ZPD) · Cultural mediation · Identity construction · Cultural repertoires · Language ideologies

L. M. Pérez Fernández, *Translanguaging in Multicultural Societies*, https://doi.org/10.1007/978-3-031-74145-6_8

8.1   Alignment of Translanguaging with Sociocultural Theories

The intersection of sociocultural theories and translanguaging unveils a rich relationship between language practices and the social context in which they occur. Sociocultural perspectives, rooted in the seminal work of theorists such as Lev Vygotsky and his followers, emphasize the crucial role of social interactions, cultural context, and shared meaning-making in shaping language development.

Within the sociocultural theories, Vygotsky's Zone of Proximal Development (ZPD) posits that individuals learn best within a range of tasks that they cannot master alone but can with the assistance of a more knowledgeable person or peer group. Translanguaging aligns with this concept by acknowledging the supportive role of multiple languages in the learning process. Learners draw upon their linguistic repertoires to scaffold understanding, utilizing the languages they are proficient in to engage with the ZPD and construct meaning collaboratively.

Moreover, the notion of cultural mediation, a cornerstone in Vygotsky's theories, finds resonance in translanguaging. Language, as a cultural tool, becomes a means of mediating knowledge, experiences, and worldviews. Consider, for example, a CLIL history lesson, where students explore the historical narrative of ancient civilizations in both Spanish and English. As the lesson unfolds, translanguaging serves as a bridge that mediates understanding among all students, regardless of their linguistic backgrounds. It becomes a conduit through which diverse cultures intermingle, facilitating mutual comprehension and shared learning experiences. Students express their ideas in more than one language, contributing diverse cultural perspectives to the discussion and collectively constructing a deeper understanding of ancient civilizations mediated by their linguistic and cultural repertoires.

Apart from aligning with the ZPD, translanguaging enhances collaborative learning within the sociocultural framework. In the context of the previous CLIL history lesson exploring ancient civilizations, translanguaging serves as a tool for collective knowledge construction. Beyond individual scaffolding, students collaboratively utilize their linguistic repertoires to approach historical concepts. As they delve into the ZPD, discussing and interpreting topics like Mesopotamian society, they are able to switch between Spanish and English when analyzing primary sources. This collective use of multiple languages becomes a social practice that enhances individual learning and cultivates a shared understanding of historical events. Therefore, from the sociocultural perspective, translanguaging is a joint effort where students collaboratively construct knowledge, drawing on the diversity of their linguistic backgrounds to deepen their comprehension of historical narratives.

Furthermore, the connection between sociocultural theories and translanguaging is evident in how they jointly contribute to identity construction in multilingual settings. Language is not merely a means of communication; it is a marker of identity, shaped by the sociocultural contexts in which it is situated. Therefore, whether in a classroom or in online interactions, translanguaging serves as a bridge for mutual understanding and contributes significantly to the collective construction of deeper understandings mediated by linguistic and cultural repertoires (Ng & Lee, 2019). Language is intimately linked to both personal and social identities, representing aspects like ethnicity, nationality, and cultural affiliations. Translanguaging becomes a tool through which individuals express their diverse identities. In diasporic communities, people might employ translanguaging practices to uphold ties with their cultural heritage while adapting to the linguistic norms of the host country. Imagine a second-generation Indian-American, born and raised in the United States, whose family maintains strong ties to their Punjabi heritage. During family gatherings and celebrations, this individual integrates Punjabi phrases and expressions into their conversations with parents and relatives, helping to preserve the richness of their cultural and linguistic heritage. However, when interacting with friends and colleagues in the United States, they effortlessly switch to English, the predominant language, to align with local linguistic norms and facilitate communication. This adept handling of languages reflects what the negotiation of their identity is like, as they bridge the gap between their ancestral culture and the cultural context of their host country.

In essence, sociocultural perspectives illuminate translanguaging as more than a linguistic phenomenon; it is a deeply social and cultural practice. Rooted in the rich soil of sociocultural theories, translanguaging embodies the collaborative, communal, and identity-driven nature of language, transcending the confines of traditional language boundaries.

8.2   TRANSLANGUAGING AND CULTURAL REPERTOIRES

One of the central aspects of sociocultural perspectives on translanguaging is the concept of cultural repertoires. Cultural repertoires encompass a wide array of linguistic resources, including vocabulary, idiomatic expressions, gestures, and cultural symbols, specific to a particular community or group. These repertoires are closely tied to the collective identity of the community, reflecting its unique heritage and shared experiences. For instance, within a bilingual community, certain idiomatic expressions might be exclusive to that community, serving as markers of belonging. Translanguaging practices within such contexts involve the smooth integration of these cultural repertoires, enriching communication and reinforcing the community's cultural identity.

Moreover, sociocultural perspectives emphasize the role of sociolinguistic norms and language ideologies in shaping translanguaging behaviors. Language ideologies refer to the beliefs, attitudes, and values attached to languages within a society (Shiffman, 1996). These ideologies influence individuals' language choices and perceptions of linguistic authenticity. In some multilingual communities, certain languages might be considered prestigious, while others are stigmatized. Translanguaging practices within such communities are influenced by these ideologies. For example, an individual might code-switch between a stigmatized regional dialect and a prestigious national language based on the social context, navigating the complex terrain of language hierarchies.

Another noteworthy dimension of sociocultural perspectives is the concept of language as a cultural resource. In multilingual societies, languages frequently embody cultural meanings and traditions. Translanguaging practices encompass leveraging these cultural resources to convey messages and emotions. For instance, during cultural celebrations, participants may utilize specific linguistic and cultural elements from various languages to express joy and unity, nurturing a shared sense of identity among those involved.

Additionally, sociocultural perspectives shed light on the role of translanguaging in intercultural communication and understanding. In multicultural societies, translanguaging practices, where individuals draw upon their linguistic repertoires, serve as a bridge for communication between diverse cultural groups, enhancing mutual understanding and dialogue. This phenomenon is normally observed in educational settings, where teachers might encourage translanguaging among students from diverse linguistic backgrounds, creating an inclusive learning environment where they can express their thoughts and ideas effectively. This idea is also linked to the concept of "culturally responsive teaching" (Carter & Bradford, 2019), which aligns with sociocultural perspectives on translanguaging. Educators who respect students' cultural and linguistic diversity create inclusive spaces. Translanguaging becomes a tool for cultural preservation, enabling students to engage with the curriculum while maintaining their heritage languages. This practice nurtures a positive sense of identity, reinforcing cultural pride and self-esteem among learners. Additionally, embracing translanguaging challenges traditional language norms. Sociocultural perspectives advocate for the acceptance of linguistic diversity, viewing translanguaging not as a deviation but as an enriching resource. Institutions promoting these perspectives favor social justice by validating the multilingual realities of individuals and communities, dismantling linguistic biases, and embracing the richness of varied linguistic expressions.

In summary, sociocultural perspectives on translanguaging practices offer a holistic understanding of the social, cultural, and identity-related dimensions of multilingual communication.

8.3 Case Study: Translanguaging in a Multilingual Classroom in Malaysia

The following case study (Rajendram, 2021) explores how translanguaging aligns with sociocultural theories, particularly in the context of a multilingual Grade 5 English language classroom in Malaysia. The study was conducted in a setting where English-only policies were enforced by teachers, yet students frequently engaged in translanguaging during their peer-to-peer interactions. These students, who were trilingual in Tamil, Malay, and English, naturally utilized all languages in their repertoire to facilitate learning, build relationships, and affirm their identities.

Over a period of six months, data were collected from 100 video recordings of students working in small groups, complemented by member-checking interviews. The study employed sociocultural discourse analysis, focusing on how learners use language in social interactions to construct knowledge collaboratively. The findings revealed that translanguaging offered significant cognitive-conceptual, planning-organizational, affective-social, and linguistic-discursive affordances, which illustrate how translanguaging serves as a critical tool for learning in a sociocultural context.

Cognitively, students used translanguaging to work through complex ideas, draw on prior knowledge, and construct new understandings together. For example, they frequently switched between languages to explain concepts, suggest ideas, and solve problems, demonstrating the deep interconnection between language use and cognitive processes. This aligns with the sociocultural perspective that learning is a social activity mediated by language, where cognitive development occurs through interaction with others (Vygotsky, 1978).

In terms of planning and organization, translanguaging enabled students to manage their collaborative tasks more effectively. They used their linguistic repertoire to negotiate roles, distribute tasks, and plan the workflow of their group activities. This aspect of translanguaging highlights its role in supporting the procedural and organizational aspects of collaborative work, which are crucial in a classroom setting where tasks require coordination and cooperation.

The study also found that translanguaging provided significant affective-social benefits. Students used it to build rapport, support each other emotionally, and engage in social interactions that strengthened their group cohesion. These interactions not only created a supportive and inclusive classroom environment but also allowed students to affirm each other's cultural and linguistic identities. The sociocultural situatedness and responsiveness of translanguaging were evident in how students wove together the personal, social, and cultural domains of their lives during their interactions. For example, they discussed their personal religious beliefs, made references to Indian and Malaysian culture, and enacted the cultural values held in high regard by their community. This reflects Canagarajah's (2007) view that language use is "a social process constantly reconstructed in sensitivity to environmental factors" (p. 94), highlighting how deeply students' linguistic practices were intertwined with their sociocultural context.

The results of this study also revealed that learners re-appropriated English, Tamil, or Malay utterances with new meanings and for new purposes. Throughout their interactions, learners engaged in a continuous process of selecting and mixing different features of the three named languages in their repertoire, often engaging in "soft assembling" these features in novel ways to suit the immediate task (García & Leiva 2014). For instance, during a riddle-writing activity inspired by

Indian folk tales, students creatively changed the pronunciation of the English word "orange" so that it mirrored the meaning of "five" in Tamil ஐந்து. Additionally, they combined English and Tamil words while adhering to English morphological rules, such as in the phrase "television பார்க்கிறான்ing" (watching television). This inventive blending of languages illustrates how learners created their own varieties of "Tanglish" and "Manglish," reflecting the dynamic and fluid nature of their linguistic practices. The study further found that students widely used the "-lah" discourse particle, a dominant feature of Malaysian dialects, creatively attaching it to English, Tamil, and Malay words to fulfill various pragmatic functions. This practice underscores how deeply embedded learners' translanguaging practices were in their sociocultural context. These findings align with Li's (2018) research on Chinese users of English, who re-appropriated English utterances to create their own version of "New Chinglish," demonstrating how language users creatively adapt language to fit their social and cultural contexts.

Linguistically, translanguaging allowed students to support each other's language development across all languages in their repertoire. They helped each other with vocabulary, grammar, and pronunciation, using their shared linguistic resources to enhance their learning outcomes. This not only supported their English language development but also helped them improve in Malay and Tamil. The use of translanguaging for these purposes demonstrates its role in building metalinguistic awareness and the ability to use linguistic features strategically in various contexts.

The findings of this study suggest that translanguaging should not be viewed merely as a pedagogical strategy but as an integral part of the learning process, deeply embedded in the social and cultural fabric of the classroom. Translanguaging in this context is more than a means to an end; it is an ongoing process through which students shape their identities, build social relationships, and engage with learning tasks.

This case study demonstrates that in multilingual classrooms, where students come from diverse linguistic and cultural backgrounds, translanguaging allows for a more holistic and effective approach to learning, making it an essential component of socioculturally responsive pedagogy. The study's findings contribute to the growing body of research that views translanguaging as central to understanding how language learning occurs in multilingual and multicultural contexts, particularly within the framework of sociocultural theory.

REFERENCES

Canagarajah, S. (2007). The ecology of global English. *International Multidisciplinary Research Journal, 1*(2), 89–100. https://doi.org/10.1080/152577 70701495299

Carter, H., & Bradford, M. (2019). Opening the window to a world wider than our little classroom. The importance of culturally relevant pedagogy. *EViE: Emerging Voices in Education, 1*(1), 18–32.

García, O., & Leiva, C. (2014). Theorizing and enacting translanguaging for social justice. In A. Blackledge & A. Creese (Eds.), *Heteroglossia as practice and pedagogy* (pp. 199–216). Springer. https://doi.org/10.1007/978-94-007-7856-6_11

Li, W. (2018). Translanguaging as a practical theory of language. *Applied Linguistics, 1*, 9–30. https://doi.org/10.1093/applin/amx039

Ng, L. L., & Lee, S. L. (2019). Translanguaging practices and identity construction of multilingual Malaysian university graduates in digital media. *English Teaching & Learning, 43*, 105–123. https://doi.org/10.1007/s42321-019-00021-6

Rajendram, S. (2021). The cognitive-conceptual, planning-organizational, affective-social and linguistic-discursive affordances of translanguaging. *Applied Linguistics Review, 14*(5), 1185–1218. https://doi.org/10.1515/applirev-2020-0075

Schiffman, H. (1996). *Linguistic culture and language policy*. Routledge.

Vygotsky, L. S. (1978). *Mind in society: The development of higher psychological processes*. Harvard University Press.

PART III

Translanguaging in Practice

CHAPTER 9

Translanguaging in Multilingual Classrooms

Abstract This chapter explores the transformative role of translanguaging in multilingual classrooms, emphasizing its integration as a pedagogical strategy to enhance language learning and promote inclusivity. It delves into various approaches, such as bridging comprehension gaps through native language use, fostering social justice by valuing students' linguistic assets, and promoting peer collaboration and multimodal learning experiences. The chapter highlights translanguaging's impact on vocabulary acquisition, confidence building, and participation among students from diverse linguistic backgrounds. It also discusses effective strategies like mediation activities, translanguaging zones, and inclusive assessment practices that support cultural and linguistic responsiveness.

Keywords Multilingual classrooms · Translanguaging · Pedagogical strategies · Language learning · Inclusivity · Social justice

In the ever-evolving domain of education, multilingual classrooms stand as vibrant microcosms of linguistic diversity and cultural richness. Within

---

L. M. Pérez Fernández, *Translanguaging in Multicultural Societies*,
https://doi.org/10.1007/978-3-031-74145-6_9

this diverse environment, translanguaging emerges as a potent pedagogical tool, bridging the gaps between languages and facilitating meaningful learning experiences. This section sheds light on the diverse ways in which educators harness translanguaging to create inclusive and effective learning environments.

9.1   Integrating Translanguaging in Language Teaching

Within the realm of language education, the incorporation of translanguaging strategies has become increasingly indispensable, aiming to recognize students' multilingual repertoires as valuable resources. This approach enables educators to create inclusive language classrooms that cater to diverse linguistic backgrounds. In this section, we will explore some approaches for integrating translanguaging into language teaching, offering practical insights for both novice and experienced educators.

Translanguaging practices can take many forms, ranging from robust to mild, depending on the extent of pedagogical intervention and the use of multiple languages in the learning process. Cenoz and Gorter (2022) describe robust translanguaging as incorporating a wide range of linguistic resources into a single lesson, promoting metalinguistic awareness and enhancing students' ability to think critically about language. Milder forms, by contrast, might involve cross-linguistic activities spread out over different lessons or subjects, helping learners make connections between languages at a more gradual pace.

Translanguaging in the language classroom transcends traditional boundaries, acknowledging students' diverse linguistic backgrounds and providing a scaffold for effective learning that can be gradually withdrawn as children become more proficient in their language skills (Lewis et al., 2012). One fundamental approach involves the strategic use of students' native languages to bridge gaps in comprehension (Ocampo, 2023). For instance, in a classroom where English is the medium of instruction, allowing students to briefly discuss key concepts in their native languages enhances understanding before transitioning back to English. This shift between languages acts as a cognitive bridge, reinforcing the learners' grasp of new vocabulary and grammatical structures.

García and Leiva (2014) argue that translanguaging functions as a tool for promoting social justice, especially in educational settings that serve language-minoritized communities. Cioè-Peña and Snell (2015) support this by stating that using translanguaging in classrooms represents a socially just act, as it transforms the perspective from viewing students' native languages as deficits to valuing them as assets. In fact, incorporating translanguaging into educational practices can change how students are perceived. For example, students with limited English proficiency might remain silent in English-only classrooms, appearing to lack progress simply because they cannot express themselves in English (Cioè-Peña & Snell, 2015). In translanguaging spaces, these students can use their home languages to aid their learning and demonstrate their understanding, becoming active members of the learning community rather than passive observers. Li (2024) further emphasizes that utilizing translanguaging as a pedagogy for inclusion and social justice requires a fundamental shift in mindset, not just practice. This shift entails adopting translanguaging pedagogy rather than merely employing translanguaging strategies. Achieving this involves processes of "co-learning" and "transpositioning," which are essential for fostering an inclusive and socially just educational environment. Transpositioning, on the one hand, involves recognizing and valuing the multiple languages and cultural contexts that students bring into the classroom. On the other hand, co-learning, as described by Li (2024), is a collaborative process where teachers and students engage as partners in the quest for knowledge, understanding, and wisdom. This approach transforms the traditional roles of teachers as dispensers of knowledge and students as passive recipients, creating a dynamic and interactive learning environment.

Furthermore, embracing translanguaging techniques encourages peer collaboration (Bisai & Singh, 2019). Group discussions that permit students to use their preferred languages facilitate lively exchanges. When students collaborate in a language they are comfortable with, their ideas flow more naturally, leading to richer discussions. In a Spanish-English bilingual classroom, for instance, students can brainstorm ideas in Spanish before collectively translating them into English, ensuring a comprehensive understanding while reinforcing language skills in both tongues. With this approach, apart from the linguistic reinforcement in both languages, students are also reminded of the importance of translating ideas rather than just words, a process that helps promote a deeper understanding of the content.

Translanguaging also significantly enhances language learners' confidence (Ha et al., 2021) and participation (Rabbidge, 2019). For students apprehensive about expressing complex thoughts in their second language, translanguaging provides a safety net allowing them to articulate their ideas in their native language before translating them, bolstering their confidence and active engagement. This approach empowers students while nurtures a supportive learning environment where language becomes a tool for expression rather than a barrier.

In language teaching, vocabulary acquisition is a fundamental aspect and the practice of translanguaging has shown remarkable efficacy in this aspect. Galante's (2020) study, conducted in English for Academic Purposes classes, specifically examined the impact of translanguaging on academic vocabulary in a multilingual context. Teachers employing translanguaging techniques observed higher scores in academic vocabulary among students compared to a traditional monolingual approach. This aligns with the idea that translanguaging transforms vocabulary building into an engaging and interconnected experience. For instance, in these lessons, learners can become aware of connections like the shared origin between the English word "restaurant" and its Spanish equivalent "restaurante." The emphasis on these connections empowers learners to leverage their existing language knowledge for more profound comprehension and retention of vocabulary in another language. Galante's findings further underline the effectiveness of translanguaging in enhancing vocabulary and promoting active engagement, thereby suggesting its potential to revolutionize language learning practices.

Moreover, integrating translanguaging extends beyond spoken language. In writing activities, students can use translanguaging to craft multilingual narratives, which can be enriched by the incorporation of phrases or expressions from their native languages, providing a cultural depth that monolingual approaches lack. This creative freedom enhances language skills and cultivates a sense of pride in students' linguistic heritage, contributing to a positive attitude toward language learning.

In expanding these ideas, recent studies by Fang et al. (2022) and Sohn et al. (2022) emphasize the importance of translanguaging in both planned pedagogical settings and content and language integrated learning (CLIL). They challenge traditional notions of "English-only" pedagogies and advocate for a more inclusive approach. Sun and Zhang's (2022) findings on the effectiveness of translanguaging in online peer feedback further underscore the benefits of incorporating translanguaging in diverse learning contexts.

Additionally, research by Steele et al. (2022) introduces the concept of transmodal assessment, emphasizing the exploration of concepts through various modes in different languages. This approach aligns with the idea that translanguaging provides students with the opportunity to express their knowledge and understanding using diverse linguistic and semiotic resources effectively.

In summary, integrating translanguaging into language teaching revolutionizes education, transforming classrooms into vibrant hubs of multilingual communication. These practices, which consider students' diverse language backgrounds, enhance language proficiency and nurture a profound appreciation for linguistic diversity, preparing students to face the globalized world with confidence and cultural fluency.

9.2 Translanguaging Pedagogies: Strategies and Best Practices

In educational settings, translanguaging in everyday interactions manifests uniquely. Students from different linguistic backgrounds collaborate on projects, engaging in peer-to-peer learning where languages intermingle naturally. This rich multilingual environment aligns with the Council of Europe's Language Passport, a tool for self-assessment that provides an overview of an individual's proficiency in various languages (Council of Europe, 2011). Moreover, a companion volume (Council of Europe, 2018) introduces descriptors that specifically address the flexible alternation between languages in comprehension and production.

In classrooms, translanguaging becomes a tool for mutual support, where students explain concepts in their native languages, enhancing comprehension among peers. Teachers, recognizing the value of students' diverse linguistic resources, create an inclusive environment where translanguaging is encouraged, favoring a sense of community and mutual respect. Translanguaging pedagogies encompass a plethora of strategies that empower educators to harness the richness of students' multilingualism. Implementing these strategies thoughtfully can transform language classrooms into spaces of exploration and understanding.

Labeling activities, for instance, are effective in both CLIL and language lessons. Educators create bilingual or multilingual labels for classroom objects, scientific equipment, or literary elements, ensuring that students encounter language in meaningful contexts. This method allows students to associate terms and concepts in multiple languages, reinforcing vocabulary and comprehension.

One translanguaging strategy that has received significant attention in the CEFR Companion Volume is "mediation," which refers to facilitating communication between speakers of different languages or those who face linguistic, cultural, or technical barriers to understanding (Council of Europe, 2018). It goes beyond simple translation by focusing on conveying meaning and enhancing comprehension in a new context. There are several types of mediation activities, each requiring a unique set of skills. The first type, "Mediating a text," involves interpreting and conveying the content of a written or spoken text to someone who cannot access the original. This can range from relaying specific information from a text to summarizing the main points and arguments in a more condensed form. The second type, "Mediating concepts," entails helping others grasp knowledge and ideas, often requiring the mediator to explain, elaborate, and stimulate discussions to facilitate conceptual understanding. The third type, "Mediating communication," aims to bridge understanding between individuals with different sociocultural or intellectual backgrounds, ensuring successful and empathetic communication. These three types of mediation activities contribute significantly to working with more than one language in the classroom helping students develop proficiency in multiple languages as well as enhancing their cognitive flexibility and cultural awareness. For instance, when students summarize a scientific article in their native language for peers, they are practicing comprehension and expression in both the language of the article and their native language. Similarly, explaining complex concepts learned in one language to classmates in another language encourages deeper understanding and retention of the material. Moreover, mediating communication between peers with different linguistic backgrounds supports a collaborative and inclusive learning environment where students learn to value linguistic and cultural diversity.

Another effective approach is the creation of translanguaging zones within the classroom which permit students to use their native languages freely while engaging in tasks. For instance, in a diverse classroom with speakers of Arabic, Chinese, and English, during group discussions, specific corners of the room can be designated for different languages with each corner representing one language. Students are encouraged to switch to their preferred language within their designated zones, enabling them to articulate ideas more comfortably in a way that respects their multilingual identities and promotes a sense of belonging and community. Similarly, in CLIL contexts, for example in a classroom of

Spanish-speaking students learning content in English, one corner can be designated for Spanish while another remains for English. Students can switch between these zones based on their comfort level, allowing them to express diverse ideas in their native language and then attempt to translate or adapt them into English. Additionally, using bilingual glossaries and concept maps can aid in content comprehension and retention. For example, when teaching a CLIL science lesson, students can create concept maps that label key terms and concepts in both English and Spanish. This helps reinforce their understanding of the material by allowing them to see connections between the languages, deepening their grasp of subject-specific vocabulary and concepts. Furthermore, implementing cross-linguistic projects, such as writing bilingual reports or creating dual-language posters, encourages students to apply their knowledge in both languages simultaneously. For instance, in a history lesson about World War II, students could create a bilingual timeline where events and descriptions are written in both English and Spanish, consolidating their understanding of the historical content while also practicing the translation of elaborate ideas between languages.

Pairing students with similar language backgrounds but different proficiency levels is an additional strategy to enhance mutual learning. Teachers can model and accept flexible language use both orally and in written assignments, creating an atmosphere that encourages experimentation with various grammatical forms. Scaffolding and utilizing exploratory talk provide space for students to test new ideas and grammatical structures, supporting the development of academic language. Providing a variety of resources in multiple languages or, if unavailable, explaining and discussing concepts in the languages spoken in the classroom, is essential. Apart from the bilingual or multilingual labels that we have already mentioned, word walls, repetition, and translation across languages can also contribute to a rich linguistic environment.

Peer teaching is another powerful translanguaging technique. Research indicates that Peer-Assisted Learning (PALM) combined with translanguaging fosters an inclusive, collaborative learning environment that enhances comprehension, presentation skills, and student well-being (Meletiadou, 2022). This approach allows students with stronger proficiency in a particular language to support peers who are still developing their skills. For instance, in a classroom where Urdu and English speakers coexist, an Urdu-speaking student can assist their English-speaking peer by explaining concepts in Urdu, then transitioning to English. This not only deepens the learner's understanding but also cultivates empathy and mutual respect. Meletiadou (2022) further notes that PALM and translanguaging provide psychological safety for students to engage in multilingual dialogue, promoting confidence and reducing language learning anxiety. Collaborative projects, such as multilingual presentations, allow students to apply their linguistic repertoires in real-world scenarios, fostering creativity, teamwork, and a deeper understanding of academic content through peer interaction.

Translanguaging journals also provide a structured platform for students to express themselves in multiple languages, akin to the already mentioned Language Passport's self-assessment (Council of Europe, 2011). Students can write journal entries, poems, or reflections using a combination of languages they are comfortable with. For instance, a student might write a reflective piece in Korean, incorporating English phrases or expressions where necessary for clarity. These journals serve as a linguistic canvas, allowing students to explore their multilingual identities and experiment with language blending, aligning with the descriptors introduced by the Council of Europe (2018). Educators can provide feedback and guidance, encouraging students to refine their translanguaging skills while expressing their thoughts authentically. Taking this a step further, educators can introduce "language exploration journals" where students engage in writing and actively explore linguistic connections. This may involve tracing the etymology of words across languages, comparing idiomatic expressions and their meanings in different languages and documenting their observations of language use in various cultural contexts, encouraging a deeper appreciation for linguistic diversity and enhancing their metalinguistic awareness. In the foreign language learning domain, another engaging activity could be "bilingual storytelling," where students create and perform stories that switch between languages, highlighting their understanding of both linguistic and cultural elements.

Multimodal projects that integrate spoken, written, and visual elements offer an excellent platform for translanguaging too. Research highlights that combining translanguaging with multimodal practices enhances communicative possibilities and engages students through various semiotic and aesthetic forms of expression (Mora et al., 2022). For instance, students can create presentations, videos, or posters that combine text, images, and spoken explanations in their native languages, allowing them to draw on their entire linguistic and semiotic repertoire. In a geography project about diverse cultures, for example, a student fluent in both Mandarin and English might include Mandarin subtitles in their presentation slides, broadening access to information. To further enhance this multimodal approach, educators could introduce "cross-cultural projects" that encourage students to explore and engage with cultural diversity, typically involving the comparison, analysis, or collaboration between different cultures. This multimodal-translanguaging approach fosters creative meaning-making and inclusivity while promoting deeper learning. Mora et al. (2022) further assert that integrating non-verbal and virtual modes of communication expands students' ability to express themselves beyond the confines of language alone.

In the context of tandem virtual exchanges, the study by Walker (2018) on German and English learners reveals a valuable strategy of using translanguaging in meaning negotiation. The learners employed translanguaging while solving language issues, negotiating roles during tasks, engaging in exploratory talk, and providing mutual support. This strategy emerged as an effective means to overcome linguistic challenges and enhance collaborative tasks within the virtual exchange setting. Furthermore, Canal's (2023) study, which focused on tandem virtual exchanges between college students at a Canadian and a Spanish university, focused on the role of learners' linguistic repertoires in learner-learner interactions. In this study, translanguaging practices were observed to occur predominantly during inquiries and explanations about linguistic aspects. The entire linguistic repertoires of the learners were essential in scaffolding conversations and facilitating understanding between participants.

To further guide educators in implementing translanguaging pedagogies, García and Li (2014) offer a comprehensive set of recommendations tailored to various language skills. For example, when students are practicing reading, they suggest assigning bilingual reading partners for collaborative assistance, providing multilingual books, and encouraging the use of diverse reading materials for research projects. For writing, their recommendations include allowing students to audio record ideas using all language resources, assigning bilingual writing partners, and promoting experimentation with translanguaging in both bilingual and monolingual writing contexts. In speaking activities, they propose assigning language partners based on proficiency levels, pairing newcomers with buddies for support, and forming groups that necessitate the use of different language resources for effective communication. Finally, in listening exercises, García and Li (2014) advocate for the creation of a multilingual listening center with varied texts and narratives, as well as encouraging students to explain concepts to each other using their diverse language resources.

Incorporating translanguaging into assessment methods contributes to equitable evaluation. Instead of restricting assessments to a single language, educators can offer options for students to demonstrate their understanding in their preferred languages. For example, in a science class, a student fluent in Spanish and English might choose to present their research findings in Spanish. By doing so, they can articulate complex scientific concepts more precisely, showcasing their knowledge effectively. This approach ensures that assessments measure content mastery rather than linguistic proficiency, promoting fairness among diverse learners. Recent studies illustrate successful integration of translanguaging into assessment design. In the linguistically diverse state of Oaxaca, Mexico, Schissel et al. (2021) conducted an action research case study with 40 pre-service language teachers, exploring a translanguaging assessment design. Their study utilized a rubric to ensure equitable assessment of multilingual students. Similarly, Lopez et al. (2017) implemented a digital classroom assessment system in US public schools, allowing emergent bilingual students to draw on their entire linguistic repertoires to demonstrate content knowledge and skills. This approach, facilitated through a computer-based testing platform, represents a practical way to advance efforts in promoting multilingualism in educational assessments. Wang and East (2023) further examined translanguaging in assessment through an online writing test for 163 absolute beginners in a Chinese as a second language program at a New Zealand university. The study found that allowing students to use their entire linguistic repertoire led to more creative and engaged digital compositions. Although some students expressed skepticism about the necessity of this approach, the study highlighted its potential to foster a more inclusive evaluation of students' abilities and validate their existing language skills as valuable resources. Another effective approach is the use of "portfolio assessments" (DeFalco, 2023), where students compile a variety of work samples demonstrating their use of multiple languages across different contexts and subjects. These portfolios can include written reflections, audio recordings of oral presentations, and multimedia projects, providing a comprehensive view of their language proficiency and growth.

In summary, translanguaging pedagogies encompass a wide array of innovative strategies that celebrate linguistic diversity and create inclusive learning environments. These practices enhance language skills and also cultivate a sense of pride in students' diverse linguistic backgrounds, promoting a positive attitude toward language learning and intercultural understanding.

9.3 BENEFITS AND CHALLENGES OF TRANSLANGUAGING IN EDUCATION

Translanguaging in education unfolds a spectrum of advantages interwoven with inherent challenges. Recognizing these aspects is pivotal, offering educators, policymakers, and researchers a realistic perspective to enhance multilingual education.

Translanguaging presents cognitive advantages, contributing to mental agility as students fluidly switch between languages, enhancing problem-solving skills and metalinguistic awareness. This linguistic flexibility nurtures critical thinking, a cornerstone of academic prowess. Additionally, the approach enriches the classroom's linguistic environment. Students draw from their diverse linguistic backgrounds, expressing sophisticated ideas and cultural subtleties precisely and accurately. This linguistic richness favors a sense of inclusivity, creating a space where each student's unique linguistic heritage is valued and respected.

Moreover, translanguaging facilitates effective communication, particularly for English language learners in CLIL settings. It acts as a bridge, allowing students to comprehend content concepts in their native languages before transitioning into English. This gradual approach ensures a smooth learning curve, boosting understanding and confidence. Beyond language, translanguaging encourages cultural appreciation since students share the customs and traditions intertwined with them, thereby developing empathy, tolerance, and a genuine appreciation for diversity.

Another notable benefit is the promotion of a positive attitude toward language learning. Translanguaging acknowledges and values students' diverse linguistic backgrounds, instilling a sense of pride in their multilingual identities. This positive outlook contributes to increased engagement and motivation, creating a conducive atmosphere for effective learning.

However, amid these advantages, educators and students encounter challenges. One key challenge is the potential resistance or misconceptions surrounding translanguaging. Some educators, parents, or policymakers may hold traditional views on language use in the classroom, viewing translanguaging as a deviation from monolingual norms. Overcoming these misconceptions requires advocacy, awareness-building, and showcasing the positive outcomes of translanguaging in diverse educational settings.

The utilization of translanguaging in assessment poses another significant challenge within the current educational sphere, dominated by the belief that assessments should primarily enhance students' educational experiences (García & Li, 2014). Standardized assessments typically adhere to a monolingual approach, creating a dilemma, particularly for bilingual students, especially those at the early stages of bilingualism. Even when multilingual summative assessments are available, students are compelled to choose a single language for responses, reflecting a monoglossic perspective of bilingualism. Despite the potential of translanguaging to revolutionize assessment practices, where students could freely demonstrate their understanding across multiple languages and modes, such adaptive tests are notably absent. The absence of translanguaged assessments raises questions about policy intentions, potentially reinforcing societal norms that marginalize bilingual practices. Although dynamic, formative assessments aligning with Vygotsky's social interactive development theory could offer a platform for translanguaging integration, reluctance persists among teachers conditioned by traditional assessment norms (García & Li, 2014). The acceptance of translanguaging in assessment demands a fundamental shift in epistemology, challenging established educational norms and necessitating a reevaluation of societal attitudes toward linguistic diversity in education. In this context, educator training becomes paramount, equipping teachers with the expertise to implement translanguaging in class demands tailored professional development programs. Additionally, parental concerns regarding language development require transparent communication. Educators must emphasize the cognitive benefits of multilingualism, assuaging fears and encouraging parental support.

Policy constraints pose another hurdle. Certain educational policies discourage languages other than the dominant one in classrooms, necessitating advocacy for inclusive language policies that recognize and support translanguaging. Resource allocation challenges, such as limited multilingual educators and teaching materials or scarcity of language assistants to provide support, exacerbate difficulties faced by students. Addressing these disparities mandates concerted efforts from educational institutions and policymakers, ensuring equitable access to resources.

In overcoming these challenges and leveraging the benefits of translanguaging, collaboration emerges as the linchpin. Creating environments that embrace linguistic and cultural diversity allows educational institutions to offer students enriching and empowering learning experiences, supporting their holistic growth—academically, linguistically, and culturally.

References

Bisai, S., & Singh, S. (2019). Bridging the divide: Collaborative learning and translanguaging in multilingual classrooms. *A Journal of Teaching English Language and Literature, 39*, 46–57.

Canals, L. (2023). Translanguaging practices and metalinguistic reflection during negotiation of meaning in tandem virtual exchanges. *Bellaterra Journal of Teaching & Learning Language & Literature, 16*(3), 1–19.

Cenoz, J., & Gorter, D. (2022). Pedagogical translanguaging and its application to language classes. *RELC Journal, 53*(2), 342–354. https://doi.org/10.1177/00336882221082751

Cioè-Peña, M., & Snell, T. (2015). Translanguaging for social justice. *Theory, Research, and Action in Urban Education, IV*(1). https://traue.commons.gc.cuny.edu/volume-iv-issue-1-fall-2015/translanguaging-for-social-justice/

Council of Europe. (2011). *The European Language Portfolio.* www.coe.int/en/web/portfolio

Council of Europe. (2018). *Common European framework of reference for languages: Learning, teaching, assessment. companion volume with new descriptors.* Council of Europe Publishing. https://rm.coe.int/cefr-companion-volume-with-new-descriptors-2018/1680787989

DeFalco, A. K. (2023). Translanguaging as a tool for equity in classroom assessment. *MinneTESOL Journal, 39*(1), 1–6.

Fang, F., Zhang, L. J., & Sah, P. K. (2022). Translanguaging in language teaching and learning: Current practices and future directions. *RELC Journal, 53*(2), 305–312. https://doi.org/10.1177/00336882221114478

Galante, A. (2020). Translanguaging for vocabulary improvement: A mixed methods study with international students in a Canadian EAP program. In T. Zhongfeng, L. Aghai, P. Sayer & J. L. Schissel (Eds.), *Envisioning TESOL*

through a translanguaging lens (pp. 93–328). Springer. https://doi.org/10.
1007/978-3-030-47031-9_14

García, O., & Leiva, C. (2014). Theorizing and enacting translanguaging for social justice. In A. Blackledge & A. Creese (Eds.), *Heteroglossia as practice and pedagogy* (pp. 199–216). Springer. https://doi.org/10.1007/978-94-007-7856-6_11

García, O., & Li, W. (2014). *Translanguaging: Language, bilingualism and education*. Palgrave Macmillan.

Ha, T. T. T., Phan, T. T. N., & Anh, T. H. (2021). The importance of translanguaging in improving fluency in speaking ability of non-english major sophomores. *Advances in Social Science, Education and Humanities Research, 621*, 338–344. https://doi.org/10.2991/assehr.k.211224.032

Lewis, G., Jones, B., & Baker, C. (2012). Translanguaging: Developing its conceptualisation and contextualisation. *Education Research and Evaluation, 18*(7), 655–670. https://doi.org/10.1080/13803611.2012.718490

Li, W. (2024). Transformative pedagogy for inclusion and social justice through translanguaging, co-learning, and transpositioning. *Language Teaching, 57*(2), 203–214. https://doi.org/10.1017/S0261444823000186

Lopez, A. A., Turkan, S., & Guzman-Orth, G. (2017). Conceptualizing the use of translanguaging in initial content assessments for newly arrived emergent bilingual students. *ETS Research Report Series, 1*, 1–12. https://doi.org/10.1002/ets2.12140

Meletiadou, E. (2022). The utilisation of peer-assisted learning/mentoring and translanguaging in higher education. *IAFOR Journal of Education: Language Learning in Education, 10*(1), 135–154.

Mora, R. A., Tian, Z., & Harman, R. (2022). Translanguaging and multimodality as flow, agency, and a new sense of advocacy in and from the Global South. *Pedagogies: An International Journal, 17*(4), 271–281. https://doi.org/10.1080/1554480X.2022.2143089

Ocampo, D. (2023). Translanguaging and reading comprehension of filipino ESL intermediate learners. *Journal of Natural Language and Linguistics, 1*(1), 13–21. https://doi.org/10.54536/jnll.v1i1.1510

Rabbidge, M. (2019). The effects of translanguaging on participation in EFL classrooms. *The Journal of Asia TEFL, 16*(4), 1305–1322. https://doi.org/10.18823/asiatefl.2019.16.4.15.1305

Schissel, J., De Korne, H., & López-Gopar, M. (2021). Grappling with translanguaging for teaching and assessment in culturally and linguistically diverse contexts: Teacher perspectives from Oaxaca, Mexico. *International Journal of Bilingual Education and Bilingualism, 24*(3), 340–356. https://doi.org/10.1080/13670050.2018.1463965

Sohn, B., dos Santos, P., & Lin, A. (2022). Translanguaging as a theory of language for a critical integration of content and language in multilingual educational settings. *RELC Journal, 53*(2), 355–370. https://doi.org/10.1177/00336882221114480

Steele, C., Dovchin, S., & Oliver, R. (2022). 'Stop measuring black kids with a white stick': Translanguaging for classroom assessment. *RELC Journal, 53*(2), 400–415. https://doi.org/10.1177/00336882221086307

Sun, P. P., & Zhang, L. J. (2022). Effects of translanguaging in online peer feedback on Chinese university English-as-a-foreign-language students' writing performance. *RELC Journal, 53*(2), 325–341. https://doi.org/10.1177/00336882221089051

Walker, U. (2018). Translanguaging: Affordances for collaborative language learning. *New Zealand Studies in Applied Linguistics, 24*(1), 1–18.

Wang, R. (2023). An analysis of the influence of French colonization on the Vietnamese education system. *Interdisciplinary Humanities and Communication Studies, 1*(1), 1–14. https://doi.org/10.61173/aj42qn74

CHAPTER 10

Translanguaging in Multicultural Communities

Abstract This chapter examines the role of translanguaging within multicultural communities worldwide. It explores how translanguaging serves as a unifying force, bridging linguistic divides and fostering cultural exchange. The chapter illustrates how translanguaging operates organically in everyday interactions, enabling effective communication and preserving cultural heritage across generations. It also examines translanguaging's impact on community development, social integration, and empowerment, highlighting its transformative potential in building inclusive and cohesive societies where linguistic diversity is celebrated as a valuable asset. Ultimately, the chapter showcases translanguaging as a powerful tool that enriches community interactions and promotes mutual understanding.

Keywords Multicultural communities · Translanguaging · Cultural exchange · Social integration · Community development · Linguistic diversity · Cultural heritage

Within the rich mosaic of multicultural communities worldwide, language serves as both a unifying force and a repository of diverse cultural heritage. From bustling urban neighborhoods where a myriad of languages collide to remote rural areas where indigenous dialects

L. M. Pérez Fernández, *Translanguaging in Multicultural Societies*, https://doi.org/10.1007/978-3-031-74145-6_10

echo through generations, this section aims to dissect the ways in which translanguaging operates, facilitating understanding and promoting cultural exchange.

10.1   Translanguaging in Community Development and Social Integration

Within multicultural communities, translanguaging reveals itself as an essential thread, weaving together the diverse linguistic strands of daily interactions. It is not merely a linguistic phenomenon but a lived experience, shaping conversations, relationships, and shared understanding among community members.

One of the most remarkable aspects of translanguaging in daily interactions is its adaptability. In multicultural communities, individuals transition between languages based on the context of their conversations. Consider a bustling marketplace where vendors negotiate prices with customers in different languages, effortlessly shifting between dialects to cater to diverse buyers. Translanguaging here becomes a practical tool, enabling effective communication and fostering a sense of belonging among community members.

Moreover, translanguaging serves as a bridge across generational divides within multicultural communities. In households where multiple languages are spoken, younger family members often serve as language brokers, translating for older relatives who might not be fluent in the dominant language. The advantage of this intergenerational exchange is that it strengthens family bonds while also preserving linguistic traditions. Through translanguaging, stories, customs, and cultural practices are shared, ensuring that the rich tapestry of heritage remains intact across generations.

Translanguaging in everyday interactions is not confined to formal spaces; it permeates the social fabric of communities. In community events, religious gatherings, and cultural celebrations, individuals freely express themselves in their preferred languages, creating a harmonious blend of voices. This communication pattern reinforces a shared sense of identity, mutual respect, and cultural pride among community members, enriching the social environment with linguistic diversity.

Moreover, translanguaging plays a key role in community development by facilitating collaboration and cooperation among individuals with diverse linguistic backgrounds. In community projects, workshops, and initiatives, the ability to integrate various languages enables a more inclusive and participatory approach. This inclusive ethos contributes to the development of a stronger and more cohesive community, where linguistic diversity is recognized as an asset rather than a barrier.

The case study of adult migrants in Yiwu, China, provides a vivid example of how translanguaging aids social integration in a superdiverse community. Yiwu, known for its international trade, attracts migrants from various countries, primarily in Africa and the Middle East. These migrants engage in learning Chinese in a new multicultural linguistic environment, where both teachers and students use translanguaging to bridge linguistic gaps and enhance mutual understanding. In Yiwu, classrooms for adult Chinese learners often become microcosms of multilingual interaction. For instance, a typical lesson might involve the teacher giving instructions in Chinese, while students discuss the material in Arabic, French, or Swahili among themselves before responding back to the teacher in Chinese (Xu, 2024). In this specific case study, we find varied ways in which teachers integrated English, Arabic, and body language to explain complex Chinese characters, ensuring comprehension across a linguistically diverse student body. One key technique was building rapport and cultivating relationships, where teachers employed their multilingual skills to create a welcoming and supportive environment, for example by greeting students in their native languages and incorporating culturally relevant expressions, so as to establish trust and facilitate deeper connections. Note-taking and memory reinforcement was another crucial technique, where students utilized translanguaging to create comprehensive, multimodal notes that included Chinese characters, pinyin, and translations in their native languages. This practice aided memory while also bridging linguistic gaps. Lastly, passing on information and behavioral management involved teachers switching between languages to convey important instructions and maintain order, ensuring that all students, regardless of their linguistic background, understood the expectations and norms. Therefore, this practice encourages students to use their full linguistic repertoire, drawing from their native languages to make sense of new concepts in Chinese, and, consequently, promoting a collaborative learning environment.

As a conduit for shared experiences, translanguaging in community development becomes a tool for empowerment. It empowers individuals to actively engage in civic activities, share their perspectives, and contribute to collective growth. This empowerment is rooted in the acknowledgment of linguistic diversity as a valuable resource that enhances problem-solving, creativity, and innovation within the community.

A crucial role of translanguaging in community development is helping people in diverse communities overcome language barriers to access essential services. Initiatives that incorporate translanguaging ensure effective communication of services, programs, and resources to all residents, regardless of their linguistic background. This approach enables active engagement in community life and empowers individuals by granting them equal access to opportunities. For instance, migrant support centers in Yiwu often employ staff who are multilingual, capable of providing information and assistance in several languages. These centers might host workshops where presentations are given in Chinese, but participants are encouraged to ask questions and share experiences in their preferred languages. This practice ensures that all community members can engage with and benefit from these services, promoting a sense of inclusion and equity (Xu, 2024).

Translanguaging acts as a catalyst for building stronger social bonds within communities. When residents can freely express themselves in their preferred languages, it creates a more authentic and comfortable social environment. This, in turn, enhances social interactions, collaboration, and a sense of unity among community members. The fluidity of translanguaging contributes to a harmonious coexistence, leading to an environment where diversity is embraced. In the previous case of migrants in Yiwu (China), outside the classroom, translanguaging continues to be a critical tool for integration and community building. Migrants use a mix of Chinese and their native languages in daily life, from shopping and accessing healthcare to participating in local events. In marketplaces, for example, it is common to hear a blend of languages as vendors and customers negotiate and socialize. A vendor might start a conversation in Chinese, switch to Arabic to clarify a point, and then use English for technical terms related to their products. This fluid language use ensures that communication barriers are minimized and that everyone can participate fully in the economic life of the community (Xu, 2024).

Furthermore, translanguaging becomes a tool for empowering marginalized groups within communities. Linguistic diversity often mirrors other forms of diversity, including socioeconomic backgrounds and cultural identities. Translanguaging provides a means for marginalized groups to voice their experiences, needs, and aspirations, ensuring that their perspectives are acknowledged and integrated into community development initiatives. Moreover, when community members express themselves in their native languages, it transcends mere linguistic communication, providing an opportunity for sharing their culture, traditions, and unique perspectives. This cultural exchange favors mutual understanding, respect, and appreciation among community members, contributing to a rich tapestry of shared experiences.

Ultimately, the application of translanguaging in community development and social integration represents a paradigm shift toward more inclusive and cohesive societies. Embracing linguistic diversity through translanguaging enriches community interactions, lays the foundation for sustainable and thriving communities, and ensures that every individual is valued and included in the collective narrative of community development.

10.2   Preserving Cultural Heritage Through Translanguaging

Amid the diverse threads of multicultural communities, the preservation of cultural heritage emerges as a paramount objective, weaving together languages, traditions, and customs in a vibrant mosaic of identity. Within these rich contexts, translanguaging is essential in safeguarding and transmitting the unique cultural legacies from one generation to the next.

One powerful avenue for this transmission is storytelling. As demonstrated in Flynn's study (2020) on transcultural and translanguaging practices in pre-school settings, storytelling serves not just as a means of entertainment but as a critical method for reinforcing cultural values and shared histories. In these settings, children engage in story circles, where they recount tales that reflect their diverse cultural backgrounds, blending languages fluidly to create narratives that resonate across different linguistic communities (Flynn, 2020). For instance, in a transcultural exchange, a child might tell a story that draws from both European fairy-tale traditions and their cultural heritage, such as incorporating a "bruja" (witch) into a familiar tale like Rapunzel, seamlessly mixing Spanish and English. This not only preserves the cultural relevance of the story but also enriches the linguistic experience for all participants.

As far as traditional practices and rituals are concerned, translanguaging acts as a bridge between the wisdom of the past and the aspirations of the future. Ceremonies, rites, and spiritual rituals, often deeply rooted in linguistic distinctions, find resonance through translanguaging. For instance, in multicultural religious settings, prayers and chants interlace languages, embodying the harmonious coexistence of diverse faiths and traditions. A notable example is the Pinoy Version New Testament, which is rendered in Taglish—a blend of English and Tagalog. This translation, completed in 2018, initially faced criticism for not adhering to standard Tagalog or English; however, it became immensely popular among Taglish speakers, demonstrating how translanguaging can effectively engage a community's spiritual needs (Del Corro, 2020).

In East Aurora (Illinois), Pastor Obe Arellano's Community Christian Church, predominantly Hispanic, initially faced challenges with bilingual Bible studies, as monolingual Spanish and English speakers struggled to communicate effectively. To address this, the church transitioned to "Spanglish" Bible studies, where Scripture was read in both languages, allowing participants to discuss the texts in any language or mix of languages they preferred (Hatcher & Son, 2022). This approach fostered a more inclusive and engaging environment, enabling congregants to express themselves freely and connect more deeply with the Scripture.

Additionally, folk music and dance, integral components of cultural expression, are kept alive through translanguaging. Musicians and dancers draw inspiration from various linguistic sources, infusing songs and performances with a variety of melodies and rhythms. In multicultural festivals, artists often integrate lyrics and tunes from different languages, creating a captivating auditory experience that resonates with audiences across linguistic backgrounds. For example, in a lively folk dance performance, participants may sing and dance to melodies that blend Swahili lyrics, Punjabi beats, and Native American drum patterns, embodying the cultural diversity of the performers. Lumban Batu and Sukamto (2020) analyzed translanguaging in Indonesian pop songs, highlighting how contemporary artists, such as Project Pop, Agnes Monica, and GAC, strategically blend Indonesian and English to convey cultural identity while appealing to global audiences. Project Pop exemplifies this fusion with their song "Dangdut is the Music of My Country," which creatively combines the energetic style of dangdut (a vibrant form of Indonesian popular music that merges local traditions with influences from South Asia and the Middle East) with contemporary themes, asserting the genre's significance in Indonesian cultural identity and its ability to evolve alongside global music trends.

Language, as a repository of traditional knowledge, finds its way into gastronomic delights. Culinary heritage, deeply entwined with linguistic labels and regional dialects, showcases the fusion of flavors through translanguaging. Recipes passed down through generations often bear multilingual imprints, reflecting the historical exchange of culinary techniques and ingredients among diverse communities. The names of dishes, in particular, reflect the amalgamation of multiple languages, illustrating the blend of culinary practices from various cultural origins. For instance, the dish "Dolma," originating in Iran, carries linguistic nuances with the term "dolmeh" derived from the Turkish word "dolma." Another example is found in the dish "Kelle Paça," translating to "heads and feet." Here, the name incorporates Persian elements, with "Kelle" signifying sheep's head, and Turkish components like "pāçe" or "pāyçe" referring to animal foot. This linguistic fusion enriches the names of these dishes reflecting the historical and cultural amalgamation present in gastronomic practices (Nikeghbal & Yüncü, 2022). Furthermore, in family gatherings, translanguaging becomes a natural mode of communication. Picture a family dinner where grandparents share cherished stories in Spanish while grandchildren respond in English, effortlessly transitioning between languages. The elders pass down traditional recipes in Spanish, preserving the culinary heritage, while younger family members translate and adapt these recipes into English, bridging the generational and linguistic gaps. Here, translanguaging becomes a means of honoring cultural traditions, ensuring they are passed down and cherished by future generations.

Moreover, in the domain of arts and crafts, translanguaging offers a canvas for creativity. Artists from multicultural communities infuse their creations with linguistic elements, whether through calligraphy, painting, or textile art. These artworks become visual narratives, blending words and images from different languages, thereby capturing the essence of cultural diversity and shared heritage. For instance, contemporary art exhibitions often feature calligraphic masterpieces that merge Arabic, Mandarin, and Indigenous scripts, creating a visual spectacle that transcends linguistic barriers and celebrates the artistic convergence of cultures. This integration of multiple languages into artistic expression not only enriches the visual experience but also reflects the dynamic and fluid nature of multilingual identities. As Futro (2023) observes, contemporary art engages with multilingualism in ways that highlight the transformative power of blending languages and artistic media, demonstrating how such practices can offer new perspectives on cultural and linguistic diversity.

In conclusion, translanguaging stands as a testament to the resilience of cultural heritage within multicultural communities. It nurtures a collective identity by interweaving languages into the fabric of traditions, ensuring that the rich diversity of cultural expression remains vibrant and evolving. As languages converge and diverge, translanguaging becomes a potent tool, preserving the diverse linguistic and cultural legacies that define the multicultural essence of communities worldwide.

REFERENCES

Del Corro, A. (2020). The Pinoy version: A revelation. *The Bible Translator, 71*(1), 18–37.

Flynn, E. (2020). "Rapunzel, Rapunzel, lanza tu pelo": Storytelling in a transcultural, translanguaging dialogic exchange. *Reading Research Quarterly, 56*(4), 643–658. https://doi.org/10.1002/rrq.367

Futro, D. (2023). *Translanguaging art: Multilingual practices of contemporary artists and their implications for language pedagogy* (PhD thesis). University of Glasgow.

Hatcher, T., & Son, S. (2022). Translanguaging: leveraging multilingualism for scripture engagement. *The Bible Translator, 73*(1), 120–140. https://doi.org/10.1177/20516770211062143

Lumban Batu, P., & Sukamto, K. (2020). Translanguaging practices in Indonesian pop songs. *ELS Journal on Interdisciplinary Studies in Humanities, 3*(2), 308–316. https://doi.org/10.34050/els-jish.v3i2.9706

Nikeghbal, N., & Yüncü, H. R. (2022). Reflection of Turkish-Persian linguistic interaction on Turkish cuisine. *Journal of Tourism and Gastronomy Studies, 10*(3), 1908–1923. https://doi.org/10.21325/jotags.2022.1073

Xu, W. (2024). Translanguaging practices and language ideologies in adult migrants' Chinese learning classrooms and beyond. *Journal of Multilingual and Multicultural Development*, 1–17. https://doi.org/10.1080/01434632.2024.2365321

CHAPTER 11

Translanguaging in Professional Settings

Abstract This chapter focuses on translanguaging in professional settings, highlighting its role in facilitating effective communication, collaboration, and innovation in globalized workplaces. It explores translanguaging's application across various sectors, emphasizing its ability to bridge linguistic barriers and enhance cultural understanding. The chapter underscores how translanguaging practices support multinational corporations in developing global strategies, improving customer service, fostering innovation in multicultural teams, and managing internal communications. Moreover, the chapter delves into how translanguaging practices improve communication between healthcare providers and patients from diverse linguistic backgrounds. It discusses the adaptation of medical terminology, the use of visual aids, and the ethical considerations of language choice in healthcare interactions. Additionally, it addresses translanguaging's ethical and legal implications, advocating for inclusive practices that respect linguistic diversity and cultural sensitivities in professional interactions.

Keywords Professional settings · Translanguaging · Globalized workplaces · Multicultural teams · Healthcare communication · Cultural understanding · Ethical considerations

L. M. Pérez Fernández, *Translanguaging in Multicultural Societies*,
https://doi.org/10.1007/978-3-031-74145-6_11

In contemporary professional settings, the use of multiple languages, often simultaneously, has become a defining characteristic of globalized workplaces. This section addresses the role of translanguaging in professional contexts, where diverse linguistic repertoires intersect, shaping communication, collaboration, and innovation. From multinational corporations to local businesses with an international clientele, the ability to manage linguistic diversity has become essential. Translanguaging practices enable effective communication, enhance intercultural collaboration, and contribute to the success of businesses and organizations in our interconnected world.

11.1   Translanguaging in the Business Sector

In the business sector, the patterns of language use in multilingual workplaces challenge conventional notions of a singular working language, often English, as suggested by Fredriksson et al. (2006). Translanguaging plays an important role in shaping global business strategies, fostering cross-cultural communication, and driving innovation. Multinational corporations, often operating in linguistically diverse environments, face distinctive contexts where effective communication is not just an advantage but a necessity for sustainable growth.

One of the key areas where translanguaging stands out is in customer service excellence, particularly in multinational e-commerce platforms, where customer service representatives proficient in multiple languages employ translanguaging techniques to enhance customer interactions. For instance, a customer inquiry initiated in Spanish could at some point transition into English, ensuring a smooth resolution process. This linguistic adaptability resolves issues efficiently creating a positive customer experience that builds trust. Creese and Blackledge (2019) underscored the significance of translanguaging in similar contexts in their ethnographic study at Birmingham's new city library, shedding light on its practical implications for enhancing communication and customer satisfaction.

Innovation in multicultural teams constitutes another arena where translanguaging encourages collaboration and creativity. Imagine a scenario within a global technology company where a diverse team of engineers collaborates on a groundbreaking project. During brainstorming sessions, team members freely switch between languages based on their comfort and expertise. This linguistic exchange ensures that diverse perspectives are integrated, leading to innovative problem-solving and product development. A study by Sun et al. (2021) supports this notion, illustrating how translanguaging practices in multinational corporations enhance team cohesion and creativity by utilizing the diverse linguistic resources of team members. Their research, conducted at a subsidiary of a German multinational company in Shanghai, revealed several translanguaging strategies adopted by local employees. These strategies included the use of key technical terms in English to maintain precision and clarity, bilingual label quests to ensure shared understanding of complex concepts across languages, cross-language recapping to facilitate detailed explanations, and cross-language alternation for seamless communication during meetings. Sun et al. (2021) concluded that translanguaging bridged communication gaps while leveraging the unique cultural insights of each team member, ultimately driving creativity and effective problem-solving within the organization.

Moreover, the management of internal communication within multinational companies is a critical aspect where translanguaging comes to the forefront. Fredriksson et al. (2006) assert that organizations with a diverse linguistic workforce often operate at the interface between several languages, creating a linguistically diverse setting. This challenges the conventional expectation of a singular working language and prompts companies to adopt strategies that embrace the fluidity of language use. The conscious ambiguity strategy, as proposed by Fredriksson et al. (2006), becomes a means of managing language diversity within organizational communication, reflecting the adaptability inherent in translanguaging practices.

Within the multicultural workplace, employees, as speakers of multiple languages with varying proficiencies, form integrated and sophisticated language systems. Angouri's (2013) exploration of workplace communication underscores this phenomenon, emphasizing that translanguaging practices are often employed to bridge communication gaps and promote mutual understanding. Employees, regardless of hierarchical status, engage in a "what works" approach when making decisions about language choice, leading to an environment where effective communication takes precedence over rigid language norms (Angouri, 2013). In addition, translanguaging proves instrumental in creating a linguistic space within the social milieu dominated by English as the common corporate language. This is evident in studies like Jonsson and Blåsjö's (2020), where professionals at two companies located in Stockholm (H&H and Verona Medical) were selected as key participants to showcase the integration of languages such as Swedish and English to accommo-date diverse communication needs. At H&H, Per, fluent in both Swedish and English, adeptly switches between languages during meetings and written correspondence to suit the context. Similarly, at Verona Medical, Richard, skilled in both Swedish and English, uses a blend of languages to ensure clarity and inclusivity in discussions and formal reports, thereby illustrating Wang and Curdt-Christiansen's (2019) notion of employees building their own language system to facilitate mutual comprehension.

Furthermore, the profound impact of translanguaging practices on advertising is evident in the strategic localization efforts of multina-tional fashion retailers. These retailers go beyond language boundaries, tailoring their advertising content meticulously to resonate with specific cultural and linguistic contexts. This approach involves crafting taglines and promotional messages that consider both linguistic characteristics and cultural sensitivities, reflecting a nuanced understanding of diverse audiences. For instance, Hidromax, a seller of swimming pools and spas, ingeniously integrates translanguaging in its advertisement, using the English phrase "The pools of the future!" followed by a different take on the Biblical reference from Ecclesiastes "algo nuevo bajo el sol" (some-thing new under the sun). This creative language blend captures the attention of a diverse audience, showcasing the retailer's adaptability and cultural awareness (Baumgardner, 2006).

In conclusion, translanguaging in the business sector serves as a linchpin for effective communication, cultural understanding, and global success. The strategic application of translanguaging transforms linguistic diversity into a powerful asset, propelling multicultural corporations toward sustainable growth and harmonious collaboration in an intercon-nected world.

11.2   Translanguaging in Healthcare Settings

In the domain of healthcare, effective communication across language boundaries is not merely a desirable skill but an essential requirement, particularly in the context of diverse linguistic and cultural backgrounds. Ortega and Prada (2020) shed light on how patients, especially within the Spanish-speaking community in the United States, incorporate English technical terms, such as /em-ar-ái/ for MRI, into their daily medical discussions, presenting a unique challenge and opportunity for healthcare professionals. This practice reflects the assimilation of English technical terms into their linguistic repertoire, reflecting a unique aspect of multicultural communication.

The necessity for healthcare professionals to comprehend community linguistic practices is underscored, as evidenced by Ortega et al.'s (2019) findings. However, the integration of these practices into medical education remains limited. As societies become increasingly multilingual, it is imperative to recognize that effective communication in healthcare extends beyond English. Brooks (2022) provides practical insights into the challenges and successes of contemporary antenatal consultations in a London hospital. The study highlights the inherent communicative features of translanguaging in heterogeneous populations, where linguistic and semiotic resources are employed for mutual comprehension. For example, Brooks describes how midwives adeptly use a blend of English and Urdu to ensure comprehensive understanding with Urdu-speaking patients during prenatal care discussions. Additionally, the study refers to instances where visual aids, such as diagrams explaining medical procedures, are combined with simplified language in English and Spanish to clarify technical or specialized concepts for patients with limited English proficiency. These examples underscore the adaptive and patient-centered approach that translanguaging fosters in healthcare settings, promoting inclusivity and effective healthcare delivery across diverse linguistic backgrounds. Exploring translanguaging in emergency situations and pharmacies further unveils its impact on patient care. Additionally, in pharmacies, where patients seek medication-related information, translanguaging becomes essential for clear and precise communication, preventing misunderstandings that may compromise patient safety.

However, challenges persist in ensuring linguistic equity. The asymmetrical nature of doctor-patient interactions, even with efforts toward linguistic and cultural accommodation, raises questions about the transformative potential of translanguaging. The decisions made by healthcare professionals, such as choosing a *lingua franca* over seeking interpreter support, underscore the contingent nature of achieving linguistic equity in practice. In addition to verbal exchanges, translanguaging profoundly influences written materials such as pamphlets, prescriptions, and health-related websites. For instance, Ishii and Takagaki (2021) highlight specific examples of how healthcare websites incorporate multilingual content to cater to diverse linguistic communities. Their study emphasizes the importance of presenting medical information in languages understood by patients, which enhances accessibility and ensures clarity in healthcare communication.

In light of these observations, it becomes imperative to address the existing gaps in the training of pre-service doctors and healthcare professionals. The conventional medical education system, which predominantly focuses on accurate monolingual medical terminology, falls short in equipping healthcare practitioners to approach the varied linguistic challenges of multicultural healthcare environments. Recognizing the value of linguistic diversity and integrating translanguaging practices into pre-service medical education will empower future healthcare professionals to adeptly address the diverse demands of language and culture. By doing so, they will be better equipped to provide patient-centered care, improving outcomes and satisfaction in the diverse and multicultural healthcare settings that characterize our modern world. Future research should focus on refining and evaluating such training programs to continually enhance the effectiveness of intercultural communication in healthcare.

11.3   LEGAL AND ETHICAL ASPECTS OF TRANSLANGUAGING IN PROFESSIONAL CONTEXTS

In the professional sphere, the integration of translanguaging practices introduces a layer of complexity to legal and ethical considerations. As linguistic diversity becomes more prominent, particularly in healthcare settings, it is imperative to closely examine the legal and ethical aspects associated with translanguaging.

From a legal perspective, the focus revolves around ensuring equitable access to information and services for individuals, regardless of their linguistic background. According to Chen et al. (2007), legal frameworks, exemplified by the actions of some US individual states, mandate the provision of language assistance services. For instance, Massachusetts enforces laws requiring emergency departments and psychiatric facilities to provide continuous access to trained interpreters, while Illinois mandates interpreters in state mental health facilities throughout the intake and evaluation process. Moreover, states like New Jersey, California, and Washington have enacted laws requiring healthcare professionals, including physicians, to undergo training or continuing education addressing language access and cultural competency. Translanguaging practices align with these legal mandates by acknowledging the diverse linguistic needs of the population and facilitating clear communication.

From an ethical perspective, the use of translanguaging practices in professional contexts should be guided by ethical principles such as confidentiality, informed consent, and respect for the client's autonomy. For example, in healthcare settings, the use of untrained interpreters or family members as interpreters can lead to ethical dilemmas, such as breaches of confidentiality and informed consent (Flores, 2005). Therefore, it is important to ensure that professional interpreters are used in situations where these principles are paramount. Additionally, translanguaging practices should be guided by the principle of respect for the client's autonomy, allowing them to choose their preferred language(s) in professional settings whenever possible, while also ensuring effective communication.

Another ethical principle that should be considered when using translanguaging practices in professional contexts is the principle of cultural sensitivity, which refers to the ability to understand and respect the cultural differences of individuals from diverse backgrounds, moving away from stereotypes and generalizations (Galanti, 2000). In professional contexts, this concept is important because it helps to avoid misunderstandings and conflicts that may arise due to cultural differences. In a scenario described by Hale (2007), a legal misunderstanding arose due to cross-cultural differences during a court proceeding involving a Central American witness. The witness, contemplating whether to allocate lottery winnings to his daughter's 15th birthday celebration or the mortgage, raised eyebrows among English-speaking court participants unfamiliar with the cultural significance of elaborate celebrations for a daughter's 15th birthday in some Latin American countries. This case underscores the importance of cultural sensitivity in professional settings. Similarly, in healthcare settings ethical translanguaging promotes understanding, enabling patients to make informed decisions about their health. It respects the patient's right to comprehend medical information thoroughly, promoting trust and cooperation between healthcare providers and patients from different linguistic backgrounds.

Finally, in educational settings, the ethical considerations surrounding translanguaging involve the principle of inclusive pedagogy which involves embracing linguistic diversity in classrooms as a hallmark of modern education and promoting an environment where students from various language backgrounds feel acknowledged and supported. Therefore, in this context, translanguaging validates students' identities and nurtures a sense of belonging, ensuring that language barriers do not hinder academic growth. This inclusive approach involves advocating for fair assessment practices that consider linguistic diversity as an asset rather than a hindrance.

In summary, ethical translanguaging practices are the cornerstone of fair, inclusive, and respectful professional interactions. Professionals across diverse fields need to approach these ethical and legal aspects with care, guaranteeing that each linguistic interaction respects the rights, dignity, and cultural aspects of all parties involved.

REFERENCES

Angouri, J. (2013). The multilingual reality of the multinational workplace: Language policy and language use. *Journal of Multilingual and Multicultural Development, 34*, 1–18. https://doi.org/10.1080/01434632.2013.807273

Baumgardner, R. J. (2006). The appeal of English in Mexican commerce. *World Englishes, 25*, 251–266. https://doi.org/10.1111/j.0083-2919.2006.00463.x

Brooks, E. (2022). Translanguaging health. *Applied Linguistics, 43*(3), 517–537. https://doi.org/10.1093/applin/amab054

Chen, A. H., Youdelman, M. K., & Brooks, J. (2007). The legal framework for language access in healthcare settings: Title VI and beyond. *Journal of General Internal Medicine, 22*(Suppl 2), 362–367. https://doi.org/10.1007/s11606-007-0366-2

Creese, A., & Blackledge, A. (2019). Translanguaging and public service encounters: Language learning in the library. *The Modern Language Journal, 103*(4), 800–814. https://doi.org/10.1111/modl.12601

Flores G. (2005). The impact of medical interpreter services on the quality of health care: a systematic review. *Medical care research and review : MCRR, 62*(3), 255–299. https://doi.org/10.1177/1077558705275416

Fredriksson, R., Barner-Rasmussen, W., & Piekkari, R. (2006). The multinational corporation as a multilingual organization: The notion of a common corporate language. *Corporate Communications, 11*(4), 406–423. https://doi.org/10.1108/13563280610713879

Galanti, G. A. (2000). *Caring for patients from different cultures: Case studies from American hospitals.* University of Pennsylvania Press.

Hale, S. (2007). *Community interpreting.* Palgrave Macmillan.

Ishii, D., & Takagaki, T. (2021). Translanguaging in healthcare websites: Implications for language policy and social cohesion. *Language and Linguistics in Oceania, 13*, 86–101.

Jonsson, C., & Blasjö, M. (2020). Translanguaging and multimodality in workplace texts and writing. *International Journal of Multilingualism, 17*(3), 361–381. https://doi.org/10.1080/14790718.2020.1766051

Ortega, P., Diamond, L., Alemán, M. A., Fatás-Cabeza, J., Magaña, D., Pazo, V., Pérez, N., Girotti, J. A., & Ríos, E. (2019). Medical Spanish standardization in U.S. medical schools: Consensus statement from a multidisciplinary expert panel. *Academic Medicine, 95*(1), 22–31. https://doi.org/10.1097/ACM.0000000000002917

Ortega, P., Prada, J. (2020). Words matter: Translanguaging in medical communication skills training. *Perspectives on Medical Education, 9*, 251–255. https://doi.org/10.1007/s40037-020-00595-z

Sun, W., Qiu, Y., & Zheng, Y. (2021). Translanguaging practices in local employees' negotiation to create linguistic space in a multilingual workplace. *Círculo De Lingüística Aplicada a La Comunicación, 86*, 31–42. https://doi.org/10.5209/clac.75493

Wang, W., & Curdt-Christiansen, X. L. (2019). Translanguaging in a Chinese-English bilingual education programme: A university-classroom ethnography. *International Journal of Bilingual Education and Bilingualism, 22*(3), 322–337. https://doi.org/10.1080/13670050.2018.1526254

Future Directions

CHAPTER 12

Translanguaging in Emerging Technologies

Abstract This chapter delves into the transformative impact of emerging technologies on language and cultural interactions, specifically focusing on Virtual Reality (VR), Augmented Reality (AR), Artificial Intelligence (AI), and machine learning (ML). These technologies are explored for their ability to facilitate multilingual communication, enhance language learning, and broaden cultural understanding. Through VR and AR applications, users engage in immersive experiences where language barriers dissolve, enabling interactive learning and cultural exploration. This chapter showcases how these innovations are reshaping global communication, fostering inclusivity, and paving the way for a more interconnected digital future where languages serve as bridges across diverse linguistic settings.

Keywords Emerging technologies · Translanguaging · Virtual Reality (VR) · Augmented Reality (AR) · Artificial Intelligence (AI) · Machine Learning (ML) · Multilingual Communication

The integration of languages and cultures is undergoing a profound transformation. As our world becomes increasingly interconnected, emerging technologies are reshaping how we communicate, learn, and interact. This

L. M. Pérez Fernández, *Translanguaging in Multicultural Societies*,
https://doi.org/10.1007/978-3-031-74145-6_12

129

chapter explores how these groundbreaking technologies intersect with the practice of translanguaging.

12.1   Translanguaging in Virtual Reality and Augmented Reality Applications

Virtual Reality (VR) and Augmented Reality (AR) have revolutionized the way we experience digital environments, providing immersive and interactive encounters. As diverse languages converge in these technologies, they create an inclusive space, breaking down linguistic barriers and fostering meaningful interactions.

In education, the fusion of translanguaging principles with VR and AR platforms presents a groundbreaking approach to language learning. These immersive tools create an environment where students can interact with diverse languages, deviating from traditional language education approaches. For instance, a teacher might design an AR lesson around everyday items, and as students scan each item, information or labels appear in various languages. This encourages students to engage with multiple languages while exploring the educational content. Some apps, such as Google AR Translate, which can instantly translate text in real time using the camera on a smartphone, are particularly useful in multilingual settings where learners can see and compare texts in different languages.

Pedagogical materials designed for VR and AR can transform traditional language learning by creating immersive, context-rich environments that naturally encourage the use of multiple languages. For instance, VR language learning applications can simulate real-life scenarios where learners must communicate in different languages. These scenarios can include virtual marketplaces, international conferences, or everyday social interactions, allowing learners to practice and apply their language skills in diverse contexts. A notable example is the ROMtels project (ROMtels, 2017), which utilized VR-like environments to support translanguaging practices among Roma students. In these spaces, learners interacted with virtual characters who communicated in a blend of English and Roma dialects, alongside Slovak or Romanian, depending on the context. Students collaborated to solve multilingual puzzles and inquiries, such as investigating historical events, while naturally blending their linguistic resources. This approach not only reinforced language skills but also honored and integrated the students' cultural and linguistic identities, showcasing the transformative potential of translanguaging in virtual environments. Similarly, the AR Language Map (Varatharaj et al., 2024) enriches language learning by enabling students to create interactive maps that depict their linguistic environments. These maps incorporate audio, video, and 3D representations of language use in various settings, highlighting how individuals engage with and utilize multiple languages in their everyday lives. The AR Language Map thus serves as a potent educational tool in combating linguistic racism and fostering empathy among students by immersively showcasing the richness of linguistic diversity.

In a similar way, cultural institutions are leveraging VR and AR to offer immersive experiences to visitors. Through these applications, translanguaging ensures accessibility and inclusivity. Historical sites, museums, and art galleries utilize AR overlays to provide translations and historical context in multiple languages. Visitors can explore exhibits and artifacts while comfortably switching between languages, deepening their appreciation of global cultural heritage. Moreover, language enthusiasts and travelers utilize VR and AR applications to explore linguistic and cultural diversity. Virtual language exchanges create authentic environments for learners to practice languages with native speakers worldwide. Translanguaging ensures the fluidity of conversations, allowing learners to refine their language skills naturally. Additionally, language tourism experiences leverage VR to virtually transport users to foreign settings, where they can interact with locals in their native languages. These virtual encounters favor cross-cultural understanding. Likewise, AR's capability to provide real-time feedback and support helps learners correct mistakes and improve their language skills on the spot, reinforcing the translanguaging process. This instant feedback mechanism is often lacking in traditional language learning, where feedback may be delayed and less contextually relevant.

Gaming experiences, too, have embraced translanguaging, enabling players to communicate effectively across linguistic divides. Multiplayer games incorporate real-time translation features, allowing gamers to collaborate, strategize, and socialize irrespective of their native languages. This enriches the storytelling experience and ensures players from diverse linguistic backgrounds can immerse themselves fully. As Arnold-Stein and Hortobágyi (2021) explain, players often engage in translanguaging by integrating gaming-specific jargon from English into their native languages. For instance, Hungarian gamers adapt terms like "damage" or "upgrade" by adding local grammatical features, creating hybrid expressions such as "damage-ot ad" ("it gives damage") or "upgrade-elek"

("I am upgrading"). These expressions are even extended to real-life contexts, such as using "raid-eljük a boltot" ("let's raid the shop") to describe a group shopping trip. In gaming, "raiding" typically refers to a coordinated effort by players to attack or explore a location to gather resources or rewards. Gamers creatively apply this term to everyday situations, humorously likening the act of shopping with friends or family to a strategic, high-stakes mission in a game. Such practices not only enrich the gaming experience but also foster linguistic creativity and cross-cultural communication within gaming communities.

In professional contexts, VR and AR applications facilitate multilingual simulations and training programs. Medical professionals, for instance, engage in virtual training sessions set in multilingual environments, nurturing collaboration and knowledge exchange. Translanguaging enables accurate communication, enhancing the training experience for participants from various linguistic backgrounds. Similarly, corporate training simulations replicate global business scenarios, preparing professionals for multilingual interactions, negotiations, and collaborative projects.

While the integration of translanguaging in VR and AR applications offers unprecedented possibilities, challenges persist. Ensuring real-time translations maintain accuracy while preserving linguistic and cultural features remains an ongoing priority for developers. To address these challenges effectively, continual efforts are made to enhance technologies through investments in natural language processing and AI-driven translations.

In conclusion, the incorporation of translanguaging in VR and AR applications represents a significant step toward a more interconnected and inclusive digital future in which technologies empower users to interact in a globalized world with languages serving as bridges that support mutual comprehension and cultural appreciation. As these applications progress, they hold the promise of a future where language barriers no longer impede meaningful interactions in the virtual sphere.

12.2   TRANSLANGUAGING IN ARTIFICIAL INTELLIGENCE AND MACHINE LEARNING INTEGRATION

The fusion of translanguaging principles with artificial intelligence (AI) and machine learning (ML) technologies has ushered in a new era of linguistic inclusivity and accessibility. As AI continues to evolve, its applications in multilingual contexts are reshaping various sectors, breaking language barriers, and facilitating global communication.

One of the most prominent applications of AI-driven translanguaging is evident in language translation and interpretation services. Platforms like Google Translate and DeepL utilize complex algorithms to translate text and speech between multiple languages. Translanguaging principles are at play here, allowing these AI systems to recognize language patterns, idiomatic expressions, and cultural particularities. For instance, these platforms can translate a colloquial phrase from Spanish into an equivalent informal phrase in English, preserving the natural flow of communication.

Furthermore, content creation, especially in social media and digital marketing, benefits significantly from AI-driven translanguaging. ML algorithms analyze audience preferences and behaviors, enabling marketers to create targeted, multilingual campaigns. For example, a global brand can adapt its advertisements to specific linguistic regions, so the content resonates culturally and linguistically with diverse audiences. Social media platforms also employ AI to facilitate multilingual content moderation, ensuring that user-generated content adheres to community guidelines across languages.

In educational spheres, AI-powered language learning platforms incorporate translanguaging techniques to provide personalized and adaptive learning experiences. These platforms assess learners' linguistic strengths and weaknesses, offering tailored exercises and feedback in multiple languages. This can be observed in language learning apps which can recognize that a user proficient in French and English struggles with Spanish grammar. The app then provides targeted lessons and explanations, integrating translanguaging to clarify concepts across languages. Duolingo, a widely-used language learning platform, employs AI to personalize lessons based on user performance and preferences (Nugraha et al., 2023). Similarly, Rosetta Stone's AI-driven platform offers immersive, contextual language practice that encourages learners to use their entire linguistic toolkit. Another didactic application involves integrating advanced voice recognition technology to allow students to practice speaking in both languages and receive instant feedback. This feature uses AI to transcribe spoken input accurately, detect pronunciation and grammar errors, and provide real-time corrections and suggestions.

Moreover, chatbots and virtual assistants have become integral parts of customer service and online interactions. AI-driven chatbots, like those found on websites and messaging apps, incorporate translanguaging techniques to understand user queries in different languages. These chatbots can engage users in multilingual conversations, providing information, assistance, and support. For example, a customer inquiring about products in Spanish on an e-commerce platform can easily interact with the chatbot, receiving responses in Spanish, enhancing user experience and customer satisfaction. In the classroom, chatbots can be used to practice speaking and writing in multiple languages. For instance, a chatbot can be programmed to understand and respond in both English and Spanish, allowing students to switch between languages as needed. Students might ask questions in English and receive explanations in Spanish or vice versa, depending on their comfort level and the complexity of the topic. This mirrors findings by Melo-Pfeifer and Araújo e Sá (2018), who observed that multilingual chat room participants utilized translanguaging to co-construct meaning, solve communicative challenges, and expand their linguistic repertoires. One advantage of these practices is that instant feedback on language use can be provided. When a student practices speaking, the chatbot uses speech recognition to provide immediate feedback that helps students improve their proficiency in both languages through an interactive and engaging approach. Another innovative approach is using platforms such as Mizou to create custom chatbots. Educators can integrate these chatbots into various aspects of their teaching to enhance student engagement and language proficiency. For example, chatbots can be programmed to initiate dialogues with students in the target language, prompting them to respond and practice conversational skills. Students can interact with the chatbot through text or voice, receiving instant feedback on pronunciation, grammar, and vocabulary usage. These chatbots can also serve as virtual tutors for writing exercises, providing detailed feedback on grammar errors, vocabulary choices, and overall coherence in multiple languages, accommodating diverse language backgrounds and enhancing comprehension.

Social robots also represent a promising avenue for integrating translanguaging practices into educational settings, particularly for language education. Their embodied presence distinguishes them from traditional technologies like tablets and computers, enhancing engagement and interaction quality in educational contexts (Van den Berghe, 2022). Equipped with capabilities for gestures that visually reinforce language meanings, social robots offer unique advantages for language learning (Rowe et al., 2013). Furthermore, in multicultural classrooms where teachers may not speak students' native languages, robots can facilitate translanguaging by pre-teaching concepts in students' first languages, providing translations, or serving as conversational partners in multilingual interactions (Van den Berghe, 2022).

In healthcare settings, AI-driven translanguaging shows promise in enhancing communication. Telemedicine platforms incorporate AI interpreters that can facilitate conversations between healthcare professionals and patients with diverse linguistic backgrounds. These systems use translanguaging to ensure precise communication, safeguarding medical terminology, and accurately conveying patients' symptoms or concerns. As Bakdash et al. (2024) highlight, advancements in AI language models provide an opportunity to address barriers in interpreter access, offering low-cost, real-time translation solutions that improve accessibility for patients. However, it's essential to acknowledge that despite the progress in AI-driven translanguaging, the human touch of traditional interpreters remains irreplaceable. Human interpreters bring a depth of cultural understanding, contextual sensitivity, and interpersonal skills that AI struggles to replicate fully.

AI technologies have also found applications in legal and administrative domains. Legal documents, contracts, and government communications often require precise translation to maintain legal validity. AI-driven translanguaging tools analyze the context and legal terminology, ensuring accurate translations across languages. This application enhances the efficiency of legal processes, enabling cross-border collaborations and international legal transactions.

In conclusion, the integration of translanguaging with AI and ML technologies represents a significant leap toward a more interconnected world. These innovations shape effective communication and enhance understanding and collaboration among diverse linguistic and cultural backgrounds. As these technologies continue to advance, they hold great promise for bridging global communication barriers and cultivating a genuinely multilingual digital environment.

REFERENCES

Arnold-Stein, R., & Hortobágyi, I. (2021). *Translanguaging, diglossia and bidialectalism in the video gamer argot. Practice and Theory in Systems of Education, 1*(2), 47–67. https://doi.org/10.52885/pah.v1i2.61

Bakdash, L., Abid, A., Gourisankar, A., & et al. (2024). Chatting beyond ChatGPT: Advancing equity through AI-driven language interpretation. *Journal of General Internal Medicine, 39*(2), 492–495. https://doi.org/10.1007/s11606-023-08497-6

Melo-Pfeifer, S., & Araújo e Sá, M. H. (2018). Multilingual interaction in chat rooms: translanguaging to learn and learning to translanguage. *International Journal of Bilingual Education and Bilingualism, 21*(7), 867–880. https://doi.org/10.1080/13670050.2018.1452895

Nugraha, D. N. S., Simatupang, E. C. M., Sari, P., Gunawan, H., Dianita, D., & Rusyan, S. (2023). Duolingo as an artificial intelligence technology-based learning system in English. *Journal Sinestesia, 13*(2), 1085–1089.

ROMtels. (2017). *ROMtels project resources. Newcastle University.* Retrieved from https://research.ncl.ac.uk/romtels/strands/wg3/wg3resources/

Rowe, M. L., Silverman, R. D., & Mullan, B. E. (2013). The role of pictures and gestures as nonverbal aids in preschoolers' word learning in a novel language. *Contemporary Educational Psychology, 38*(2), 109–117. https://doi.org/10.1016/j.cedpsych.2012.12.001

Van den Berghe, R. (2022). Social robots in a translanguaging pedagogy: A review to identify opportunities for robot-assisted (language) learning. *Frontiers in Robotics and AI, 9*, 1–8. https://doi.org/10.3389/frobt.2022.958624

Varatharaj, A., Welch, A., Bucholtz, M., & Lee, J. S. (2024). Teaching linguistic justice through augmented reality. *arXiv e-prints, 1*(1), 1–7. https://arxiv.org/pdf/2404.12563

CHAPTER 13

Translanguaging in Linguistic Preservation

Abstract This chapter explores how translanguaging practices serve as a crucial strategy for the preservation and revitalization of endangered languages amid the pressures of globalization. It examines translanguaging's role in indigenous language preservation efforts, emphasizing its capacity to create inclusive educational environments where minority languages can thrive alongside dominant languages. Through case studies and research, the chapter illustrates how translanguaging promotes intergenerational language transmission, fosters cultural identity, and supports sustainable language use within indigenous communities. Additionally, it discusses pedagogical approaches that integrate translanguaging to enhance language learning outcomes and empower speakers of minoritized languages, highlighting its transformative potential in educational contexts worldwide.

Keywords Linguistic preservation · Translanguaging · Endangered languages · Indigenous language revitalization · Cultural identity · Intergenerational transmission · Inclusive education

Language, as a repository of collective wisdom, stories and traditions, holds the essence of a community's identity. In the face of globalization's advancement, numerous languages worldwide hover on the verge

© The Author(s), under exclusive license to Springer Nature   137
Switzerland AG 2024
L. M. Pérez Fernández, *Translanguaging in Multicultural Societies*,
https://doi.org/10.1007/978-3-031-74145-6_13

of extinction, threatening the unique heritage they embody. Translanguaging practices offer a potential lifeline in this scenario, facilitating the preservation of linguistic diversity by encouraging communication across language boundaries.

13.1   THE ROLE OF TRANSLANGUAGING
IN THE PRESERVATION OF INDIGENOUS LANGUAGES

Language revitalization and preservation efforts within indigenous communities are paramount for safeguarding cultural heritage. The incorporation of translanguaging principles, as highlighted by Seals and Olsen-Reeder's (2020) study, serves as a crucial aspect of this broader initiative by offering a responsive framework that addresses the specific concerns faced by indigenous languages.

Sustainable translanguaging, as conceptualized by Cenoz and Gorter (2017), provides a comprehensive approach to language revitalization that ensures a positive impact on minority language maintenance. This approach delineates clear guiding principles, ensuring that translanguaging practices actively support, rather than undermine, efforts to maintain and preserve indigenous languages. The first principle emphasizes the creation of "breathing spaces" within educational environments where the minority language can be freely spoken without the overshadowing influence of majority languages. This concept, reminiscent of Fishman's notion (1991), suggests designated areas or classrooms where the minority language can thrive independently, an approach that contrasts with traditional language isolation practices by integrating pedagogical strategies that support translanguaging across various educational contexts. Furthermore, Cenoz and Gorter's (2017) second principle emphasizes the development of the need to use the minority language through translanguaging which helps in organically integrating the language into various aspects of daily life, reinforcing its importance. They illustrate this with examples from the Basque Country, where bilingual speakers alternate between Basque and Spanish in official speeches, requiring comprehension of both languages to fully understand the discourse. This intentional use of translanguaging highlights the functional value of the minority language and promotes its active use in everyday contexts, contributing to a deeper linguistic integration and comprehension among speakers. The third principle underscores the importance of leveraging emergent multilinguals' resources to reinforce all languages and develop metalinguistic awareness. This involves encouraging students to draw upon their entire linguistic repertoire to enhance their understanding of languages and content, aligning with Cummins (2007) and Cenoz and Gorter's (2015) frameworks for multilingual education. Additionally, the fourth principle focuses on enhancing language awareness by exploring students' knowledge of the social status, functioning, and language practices within society. This awareness contributes to a deeper understanding of the role of minority languages and supports the development of multilingual identities among students from diverse linguistic backgrounds. Finally, the fifth principle emphasizes the link between spontaneous and pedagogical translanguaging practices, particularly crucial for regional minority languages. Schools are encouraged to recognize and build upon students' spontaneous translanguaging practices, thereby supporting the development of basic communicative skills and fostering linguistic identity formation.

The integration of sustainable translanguaging practices in indigenous language revitalization efforts extends beyond theoretical frameworks, finding practical application in real-world educational settings. Seals and Olsen-Reeder's (2020) study provides insightful findings on spontaneous translanguaging, showcasing its normalcy in daily interactions within educational spaces like the puna reo. Both teachers and students engage in receptive and productive communication through translanguaging, demonstrating the acceptability and support for utilizing their complete linguistic resources. This natural integration of translanguaging aligns with the sustainable framework, emphasizing the importance of designing functional spaces for the minority language.

Similarly, Zavala (2015) examines Quechua education for emergent bilinguals in urban schools, contributing to the execution of a language policy aimed at encouraging the use of Quechua in the Peruvian Andes. This is illustrated in the real case study of Silvia, an urban teacher with no formal training in Indigenous Bilingual Education (IBE) or Quechua literacy, embarked on teaching Quechua spontaneously. Her decision stemmed from personal connections rather than academic motivations. Raised in a Spanish-speaking environment despite having Quechua-speaking parents, she rediscovered her heritage through interactions with her grandmother. Reflecting on her parents' discrimination for speaking Quechua, she felt compelled to revive the language, despite initial inadequacies acknowledged by Quechua experts. Initially aiming for a purist approach by teaching exclusively in Quechua, Silvia later embraced a translanguaging approach due to the practical need to communicate effectively with students. Her classroom became a space where both Quechua-speaking and Spanish-speaking students engaged, challenging the dichotomy typically drawn between the two languages in educational settings. Silvia's pedagogy emphasized critical language awareness, encouraging students to reflect on the sociopolitical dimensions of language use and her strategy involved using both Quechua and Spanish interchangeably, depending on the students' proficiency and the context of communication. This flexible approach aimed to generate a positive attitude toward Quechua, ensuring that all students, regardless of their initial proficiency, felt valued within the classroom community. She actively challenged the notion that only fluent Quechua speakers were legitimate, celebrating efforts to speak and engage with the language. In her classroom, Silvia employed repair strategies when students responded in Spanish, encouraging them to rephrase their answers in Quechua and validating their attempts at using it while promoting a sense of belonging among those less fluent. Through such practices, she sought to empower students, particularly those from rural backgrounds with high Quechua proficiency, who often faced marginalization in urban educational settings. Over time, Silvia observed a transformation among her students who, initially, were hesitant to speak Quechua due to historical stigmatization and gradually embraced the language with pride. This shift was evident as students began helping each other in Quechua tasks and discussing Quechua among themselves positively making the classroom become a space where linguistic diversity was valued and students gained confidence in their bilingual abilities. However, Silvia's approach to teaching Quechua was not without challenges. Many Quechua experts questioned her method of translanguaging, advocating for a more rigid approach emphasizing grammatical correctness and formal conventions. Despite this skepticism, Silvia remained convinced that translanguaging was the most effective strategy in her context as she believed it enhanced students' inclusion, motivation and understanding, creating a safe and respectful environment where all students felt part of a community of legitimate Quechua speakers.

Wigglesworth's study (2020), already mentioned in Chapter 5, provides another compelling example of how translanguaging can support Indigenous language preservation. Conducted in remote Indigenous communities in Australia, where Standard Australian English is the school language but not the language used at home, the research focused on Indigenous children who come to school with minimal knowledge of English but speak two or more local languages, creole, or Aboriginal English. These children often face linguistic challenges in the classroom due to the mismatch between their home languages and the standard school language. Wigglesworth (2020) advocates for the use of translanguaging techniques in the classroom to support these students so as to help students engage in exploratory talk, enhance their understanding of classroom activities, and promote discussions that bridge Western educational practices with Indigenous ways of knowing.

In indigenous communities, the role of translanguaging extends to community engagement and broader sociocultural contexts. Functional spaces that encourage the use of the minority language transition from educational environments to community centers, cultural events, and gatherings, becoming linguistic ecosystems fostering continual language use. Additionally, translanguaging promotes intergenerational dialogue within indigenous communities. Fluent elders converse with younger generations who predominantly speak the dominant language, utilizing translanguaging as a bridge for communication and understanding. These dialogues are essential for passing down cultural traditions, stories, and rituals, ensuring the continuity of indigenous heritage. Wang's study (2022) in New Zealand provides a pertinent example of how translanguaging operates within a mainstream educational context while integrating indigenous epistemologies, which "denote any knowledge traditionally held by Indigenous peoples and communities" (Wang, 2022, p. 7). In this study, students enrolled in a beginning Chinese course were tasked with creating video projects that introduced their families and they were encouraged to employ both Chinese and Māori languages organically, reflecting their familial and cultural backgrounds. The vlogs were assessed not only on language proficiency but also on how well students integrated Māori cultural elements into their presentations. Through this project, students demonstrated a deep connection to their cultural roots and engaged in critical reflections on the cultural underpinnings of the languages they were learning. As Wang (2022) points out, they noted significant similarities and differences between Chinese and Indigenous cultures, particularly in their emphasis on genealogy and familial relationships. For instance, Chinese culture places importance on ancestral honor through the order of family names preceding given names, whereas Māori cultural practices in self-introduction similarly honor ancestry but often emphasize natural landmarks like mountains or rivers associated with ancestral origins.

Furthermore, Kleeman (2021) provides a significant case study on the application of translanguaging within early childhood education focusing on the Sámi people, an indigenous group native to the Sápmi region encompassing parts of Norway, Sweden, Finland, and Russia. Historically marginalized, the Sámi languages face endangerment, a concern addressed in Sámi kindergartens where children aged 4–5, though understanding Sámi, showed limited spontaneous use. The intervention aimed to ensure Sámi language preservation through various translanguaging strategies, with a key focus on creating the already mentioned "breathing spaces" (Fishman, 1991), which could provide intentional contexts and opportunities where Sámi language and culture are actively promoted and practiced, countering the dominance of Norwegian and other majority languages. Firstly, teachers employed multilingual modeling during outdoor activities such as berry picking. Using a GoPro camera, they demonstrated language use in both Norwegian and North Sámi, guiding children through the process of identifying ripe berries, discussing their names in both languages, and recording these activities. The camera served as a tool for teachers to explain tasks and narrate in both languages while filming, encouraging children to describe their actions and discoveries in either language they felt comfortable with, thereby integrating Sámi into everyday activities. Secondly, during campfire sessions, teachers engaged children in the culturally significant activity of storytelling, which is widely practiced in northern Norwegian kindergartens. Sitting around the campfire, teachers created an atmosphere conducive to using both Norwegian and North Sámi languages naturally, using short, common phrases such as imperatives ("come here," "look at that," "wait a little") typical in kindergarten settings and child-directed speech. They employed these phrases to support emerging bilingualism, with frequent confirmation of utterances in both languages and the use of body language to reinforce activities. This approach included code-switching, where teachers repeated phrases in a new language to encourage participation, through a collaborative approach to language learning. They also sought affirmation regarding pronunciation and semantics, promoting metalinguistic awareness. Thirdly, teachers led circle time planned sessions that are a core part of the kindergarten's approach. They used visual aids like photos of children picking berries and images of different berries and heather. The focus was on engaging discussions about greetings and the berry forest, using both Sámi and Norwegian languages. Teachers prompted the children to participate by asking questions and encouraging responses in either language. They ensured everyone understood concepts like morning time and the location in the berry forest by switching between Sámi and Norwegian as needed. This approach helped the children learn vocabulary and phrases naturally while connecting them to Sámi language and culture in everyday activities at the kindergarten. The results showed that children displayed positive attitudes toward their cultural identity and greater confidence in using their linguistic repertoires. This focus on early childhood education is particularly noteworthy, as it emphasizes the importance of integrating translanguaging practices from a young age, thereby establishing a strong foundation for the sustainability of indigenous languages like Sámi.

In essence, translanguaging in language preservation efforts becomes more than a linguistic practice; it becomes a lifeline for endangered indigenous languages. Embracing translanguaging allows indigenous communities to craft living languages that adapt to contemporary contexts while honoring their rich cultural legacy. These endeavors, which safeguard linguistic diversity and reinforce indigenous identity, ensure that the echoes of the past resonate strongly in the hearts and minds of future generations.

13.2 Pedagogical Translanguaging and Minoritized Languages Revitalization

Language revitalization efforts in minoritized communities aim to address decreasing speaker numbers and prevent further linguistic decline. These efforts acknowledge the interconnection among sociopolitical factors influencing language development (Liddicoat & Bryant, 2001). In this context, translanguaging emerges as a pedagogical strategy with the potential to contribute significantly to language revitalization.

Within transformative pedagogy, translanguaging stands out as a potent substitute for conventional methods, which frequently struggle to effectively tackle the hurdles encountered by minoritized languages. Peach-Hughes (2022)' study contributes valuable perspectives on school education in minority language revitalization, focusing on Gaelic Medium Education (GME) in Scotland. In her study, she underscores the dominance of English in children's lives, highlighting the challenges and opportunities in recent revitalization efforts. She advocates for a subtle and detailed approach, incorporating translanguaging pedagogies to effectively revitalize Gaelic, especially considering the complexities revealed by Dunmore's (2018) research on the decline of Gaelic language speakers in Scotland.

In Spain, Basque-medium education significantly shapes the growth of Basque speakers (Leonet et al., 2017). In the Basque Autonomous Community (BAC), the Sociolinguistic Survey is conducted every five years to examine the use of Basque and Spanish among the population aged 16 and over. This survey, which covers approximately 2,680,000 people, provides crucial data on the vitality and change of languages in the region. According to the 2021 Sociolinguistic Survey (Basque Government, 2021), the most recent to date, 36.2% of the population aged 16 and over are active Basque speakers, meaning that they use Basque as much or more than Spanish in their daily lives. Additionally, 18.6% are passive Basque speakers, who have passive knowledge of Basque but do not actively use it in their daily lives. Furthermore, 45.3% are Spanish speakers, who primarily use Spanish. These figures reflect a significant increase in the number of active Basque speakers in recent decades, especially among young people aged 16–24, where 74.5% actively use Basque, in comparison with 25% in 1991, indicating a notable shift in language use in the region. The effectiveness of Basque-medium education in encouraging this growth is well illustrated in a specific intervention, which took place in a public school within the BAC, part of the Amara Berri system, involving over 600 students from lower and middle socioeconomic classes (Leonet et al., 2017). This pedagogical approach aimed to enhance language awareness and proficiency across Basque, Spanish, and English, implemented through translanguaging pedagogies. During the intervention, students worked in groups within designated areas of the classroom, using translanguaging materials that integrated all three languages. Activities ranged from analyzing the languages present in their town to writing narrative texts in Basque, Spanish, and English with the objective of promoting metalinguistic awareness as well as facilitating the natural use of multiple languages in communicative settings. The type of activities provided opportunities for students to compare and contrast language use in different contexts and helped them realize that they could apply similar narrative structures and storytelling techniques across languages, adapting them to the specific linguistic norms of each. While teachers involved in the intervention initially expressed concerns about maintaining the prominence of Basque within the curriculum, they also noted various benefits of translanguaging pedagogies since students' proficiency and confidence in using Basque improved significantly. Teachers also reported that students who had previously been passive Basque speakers became more actively engaged in using the language across different classroom activities.

In a broader context, Burton and Rajendram (2019) emphasize the far-reaching implications of educators' stances on multilingual classroom practices, particularly how their perspectives on translanguaging are influenced by beliefs about language development, personal language learning experiences, and institutional constraints, resulting in differing views on whether it is a resource for learning or an obstacle to developing English proficiency. This is echoed by Maseko's (2022) findings, which show that teachers' orientations toward translanguaging—specifically whether they embrace or resist it—directly influence the agency of minoritised languages in the classroom. Maseko argues that teachers who align with minoritised languages (language concordant) foster environments that support translanguaging, thereby empowering students and challenging monolingual practices. In contrast, teachers who are indifferent or resistant to translanguaging (language discordant) limit opportunities for minoritised language revitalization. Sayer (2013) further contributes to this discourse by examining the use of translanguaging in a bilingual classroom with Latino students in San Antonio, Texas. In this setting, teachers use translanguaging to address students' identity challenges, foster cultural integration, and support linguistic development. A key focus of Sayer's study is how students, whose home language is often TexMex—a vernacular variety of Spanish mixed with English—engage with the academic space. TexMex is distinct from both Standard Spanish and Standard English, and it carries its own unique features, such as specific lexical choices, code-switching, and syntax that reflect the interplay between both languages. In Sayer's observations, Ms. Casillas, a teacher in the study, encourages students to use their language repertoire as a means of engaging with and expressing their Tejano identity. In one instance, during a lesson on compound words, the class quickly diverges from the academic content into a broader discussion about cultural practices, such as sunbathing. As students debate why Latinos don't typically engage in sunbathing, they mix English and Spanish, creating a space where their language choice is linked to personal and cultural identity. Ms. Casillas, recognizing the potential for deeper learning, guides the students back to the lesson while reinforcing the importance of embracing their skin color and cultural background. Here, language use becomes a powerful tool for cultural affirmation, with TexMex acting as a bridge between students' everyday lives and academic content.

In line with this perspective, Portolés and Martí (2017) investigate translanguaging practices within an English as an Additional Language (EAL) classroom, in a school where Catalan serves as the primary medium of instruction. Over the course of an academic year, Portolés and Martí conducted qualitative research involving extensive classroom observations. They focused on how young learners (ages 4–5) interacted using Catalan, Spanish, and English. Despite English being predominant (accounting for 83% of classroom discourse), Catalan (13%) and Spanish (4%) also played significant roles. Their findings reveal specific instances of translanguaging functions employed by the students. One of the prominent functions observed was the use of translanguaging to mediate understandings. This involved students interpreting and explaining concepts in different languages to aid comprehension among peers. For example, in classroom interactions, students would switch between languages to ensure everyone understood instructions or concepts presented by the teacher. In the example provided, the teacher instructs a specific student to be quiet, but he continues speaking despite the instruction. Another student intervenes by using Catalan to interpret and explain the teacher's message to him by saying "La mestra diu que te calles" (The teacher tells you to be quiet), providing a direct translation and interpretation of the teacher's command. Likewise, the study highlighted how young learners often use their multilingual abilities to include or exclude others in classroom activities, for example by interrupting in Spanish to ask if they and another person can also participate, demonstrating a desire to be included in the activity. Conversely, they might use another language to comment that someone has already made a choice, potentially excluding them from further participation or consideration. These instances illustrate how translanguaging serves as a means to shape social interactions within educational settings. Additionally, translanguaging served as a means for students to demonstrate knowledge, often by explaining concepts or answering questions in different languages based on their familiarity and comfort level. In the example provided by Portolés and Martí (2017), the teacher initiates a conversation by asking a student if they know what the color black is. The student responds by stating, "black es un color en inglés" (Black is a color in English), which demonstrates the student's ability to use translanguaging to explain a concept in English using Spanish. The teacher reacts with an "ah!" indicating acknowledgment and curiosity and the student further elaborates, "yo lo sé porque un día me lo dijo mi tete" (I know it because my bro told me), integrating personal experience and family relationships into their explanation. The teacher then acknowledges this by repeating the correct English term, "yes (.) black, this is colour black." Finally, another significant function identified was the role of translanguaging in co-constructing meanings, which refers to how young learners use their existing linguistic knowledge to create new understandings and establish connections between different languages. During a classroom activity, the teacher asks a student about the color of a skirt. The student responds with "blau," which is Catalan for blue. The teacher repeats "blau" with exaggerated intonation, prompting the student to clarify that "blau" is used in Catalan, while "blue" is the appropriate term in English. This interaction showcases how the student, who is of Moroccan origin and learning multiple languages including Arabic, Catalan, Spanish, and English, engages in translanguaging to communicate effectively. According to Portolés and Martí (2017), such moments are valuable for learning because they encourage students to explore linguistic connections and deepen their metalinguistic awareness. They even suggest that the teacher could have expanded on this interaction by discussing how the word "blue" in English relates to "blau" in Catalan, "bleu" in French, "blu" in Italian, and "azul" in Spanish, which originates from Arabic thereby integrating other languages that are present in students' linguistic repertoires (like Arabic in this case). Such translanguaging practices are crucial for supporting language acquisition and revitalizing minoritized languages by integrating them naturally into daily classroom activities.

Duarte's (2018) study contributes further to our understanding of translanguaging in multilingual settings, focusing on Luxembourg and the Netherlands. The study involved design-based research projects in these two distinct settings to operationalize translanguaging as a pedagogical approach for including migrant and minority languages in mainstream education. In Luxembourg, the study focused on pre-school education where teachers sought to bridge the linguistic gap between Luxembourgish and Portuguese-speaking pupils. Luxembourg is characterized by its multilingual population, with Luxembourgish, French, and German as official languages and a significant Portuguese-speaking community. Translanguaging was implemented in two main ways: pedagogical translanguaging and spontaneous translanguaging. Pedagogical translanguaging involved systematic activities planned for three hours a week, during which a Portuguese teacher co-taught with a Luxembourgish teacher. This structured approach aimed to integrate Portuguese and Luxembourgish in a controlled manner. Spontaneous translanguaging, on the other hand, encouraged fluid discursive practices among students, allowing them to use their home languages during peer interactions to cognitively engage with new content. These spontaneous moments often occurred during planned pedagogical translanguaging sessions, creating a more inclusive classroom environment. An illustrative example from the study involves a pre-school class where the teacher facilitated learning by discussing ingredients used for baking in both Luxembourgish and Portuguese. When discussing the location of flour among visually similar ingredients, the Luxembourgish-speaking teacher prompted Portuguese-speaking students to provide the Portuguese word for "flour" (*farinha*) enhancing their understanding of both content and language through translanguaging practices. This intervention underscored how translanguaging serves both symbolic and epistemological functions in the classroom. Symbolically, it acknowledges and integrates students' linguistic assets, creating a more inclusive educational environment. Epistemologically, translanguaging supports cognitive processing by reinforcing understanding across languages and content areas, thereby enhancing bilingual proficiency and retention.

In the Netherlands, the study centered on primary education in Friesland, an officially bilingual province in the North of the Netherlands, where Dutch coexists in a diglossic situation with West Frisian, a Germanic language that is the second official language of the country. In response to the region's multilingualism, trilingual schools were established, offering instruction in Dutch, English, and Frisian. These schools employ a triple-immersion approach, dedicating different days of the week to each language. Duarte's (2018) intervention took place in classrooms with pupils aged 7–12 years. In them, translanguaging was used to create moments of less language separation, alternating languages within a single class. Teachers provided new input in the language in which pupils were less proficient, and then had pupils discuss content and language with peers in another language. An illustrative example from a second-grade classroom shows how translanguaging was integrated into daily routines. The sequence started with morning greetings in Frisian, Dutch, English, Polish, and Arabic. This routine practice helped create a multilingual environment. The teacher managed the activity in Frisian, asking pupils to recite the days of the week and count up to fourteen in the three school languages. Polish and Arabic speaking pupils were then asked to count in their home languages, receiving positive reinforcement from the teacher. The teacher explained cultural differences in counting methods (such as that in Arabic, counting typically starts with the little finger, which contrasts with the counting method familiar to other pupils) engaging with pupils primarily in Frisian. Two primary functions of translanguaging were identified in this intervention. First, it acted as a bridge between the main language of instruction for the day (Frisian) and the other two instructional languages (Dutch and English), effectively breaking down traditional language compartmentalization. This approach contrasts with Cummins' (2008) concept of "language solitude," which involves the separation of languages in educational settings. Second, translanguaging was used as a scaffold to link knowledge in the three instruction languages to the home languages (Polish and Arabic), an approach that enhanced pupils' engagement and built connections between their home and school languages.

However, recent research on translanguaging in contexts focused on minoritized language maintenance, particularly examining Javanese in Indonesia, offers a contrasting viewpoint (Margana & Rasman, 2021). This study highlights significant challenges in implementing translanguaging within educational settings where majoritized languages like English and Indonesian dominate. Despite translanguaging's potential benefits for sustaining minoritized languages, existing language inequalities often hinder its effectiveness. Students' preferences for majority languages due to societal ideologies may further complicate efforts to promote and maintain minoritized languages like Javanese through translanguaging practices (Margana & Rasman, 2021). These findings suggest the importance of developing context-specific strategies to support linguistic diversity and revitalization efforts in educational settings.

In conclusion, the amalgamation of pedagogical translanguaging with revitalization efforts becomes a catalyst for change, offering a culturally sensitive approach to the diverse challenges faced by minoritized languages. This symbiotic relationship between pedagogical strategies and language revitalization underscores the need for tailored approaches that address linguistic aspects while considering the sociopolitical contexts in which these languages exist. Needless to say that educators play a central role in this process, as their engagement in translanguaging practices becomes instrumental in challenging existing paradigms and paving the way for the legitimization and revitalization of minoritized languages. Through such transformative practices, pedagogical translanguaging emerges as a beacon of hope, providing a pathway toward linguistic diversity and vitality in the face of linguistic decline.

References

Basque Government. (2021). *VII Encuesta Sociolingüística 2021* [The Sociolinguistic Survey of the Basque Autonomous Community]. Department of Culture and Language Policy of the Basque Government. https://www.eustat.eus/elementos/ele0021500/vii-encuesta-socioling
uistica/inf0021552_c.pdf

Burton, J., & Rajendram, S. (2019). Translanguaging-as-Resource: University ESL Instructors' Language Orientations and Attitudes Toward Translanguaging. *TESL Canada Journal, 36*(1), 21–47. https://doi.org/10.18806/tesl.v36i1.1301

Cenoz, J., & Gorter, D. (2015). Towards a holistic approach in the study of multilingual education. In J. Cenoz & D. Gorter (Eds.), *Multilingual education: Between language learning and translanguaging* (pp. 1–15). Cambridge University Press.

Cenoz, J., & Gorter, D. (2017). Minority languages and sustainable translanguaging: Threat or opportunity? *Journal of Multilingual and Multicultural Development, 38*, 901–912. https://doi.org/10.1080/01434632.2017.1284855

Cummins, J. (2007). Rethinking monolingual instructional strategies in multilingual classrooms. *Canadian Journal of Applied Linguistics, 10*, 221–240.

Cummins, J. (2008). Teaching for transfer: Challenging the two solitudes assumptions in bilingual education. In N. H. Hornberger (Ed.), *Encyclopedia of language and education* (pp. 1528–1538). Springer.

Duarte, J. (2018). Translanguaging in the context of mainstream multilingual education. *International Journal of Multilingualism, 17*(2), 232–247. https://doi.org/10.1080/14790718.2018.1512607

Dunmore, S. (2018). When school is over and done with: Linguistic practices and sociodemographic profiles of Gaelic-medium educated adults. In C. Smith-Christmas, & M. MacLeod (Eds.), *Gaelic in contemporary Scotland: The revitalisation of an endangered language* (pp. 62–78). Edinburgh University Press.

Fishman, J. A. (1991). *Reversing language shift: Theoretical and empirical foundations of assistance to threatened languages*. Multilingual Matters.

Kleeman, C. (2021). Pedagogical translanguaging to create sustainable minority language practices in kindergarten. *Sustainability, 13*(7), 1–19. https://doi.org/10.3390/su13073613

Leonet, O., Cenoz, J., & Gorter, D. (2017). Challenging minority language isolation: Translanguaging in a trilingual school in the Basque Country. *Journal of Language, Identity & Education, 16*(4), 216–227. https://doi.org/10.1080/15348458.2017.1328281

Liddicoat, A. J., & Bryant, P. (2001). Language planning and language revival: A current issue in language planning. *Current Issues in Language Planning, 2*(2–3), 137–140. https://doi.org/10.1080/14664200108668022

Margana., & Rasman. (2021). Translanguaging and minoritized language maintenance: Lessons from Indonesia. *3L: Language, Linguistics, Literature. The Southeast Asian Journal of English Language Studies, 27*(2), 1–15. https://doi.org/10.17576/3L-2021-2702-01

Maseko, B. (2022). Translanguaging and minoritised language revitalisation in multilingual classrooms: Examining teachers' agency. *Southern African Linguistics and Applied Language Studies, 40*(2), 1–15. https://doi.org/10.2989/16073614.2022.2040370

Peach-Hughes, T. (2022). Minority language education: Reconciling the tensions of language revitalisation and the benefits of bilingualism. *Children's Social & Economic Studies, 36*(3), 336–353. https://doi.org/10.1111/chso.12537

Portolés, L., & Martí, O. (2017). Translanguaging as a teaching resource in early language learning of English as an additional language (EAL). *Bellaterra Journal of Teaching & Learning Language & Literature, 10*(1), 61–77. https://doi.org/10.5565/rev/jtl3.698

Sayer, P. (2013). Translanguaging, TexMex, and bilingual pedagogy: Emergent bilinguals learning through the vernacular. *TESOL Quarterly, 47*(1), 63–88. https://doi.org/10.1002/tesq.53

Seals, C. A., & Olsen-Reeder, V. (2020). Translanguaging in conjunction with language revitalization. *System, 92*, 1–11. https://doi.org/10.1016/j.system.2020.102277

Wang, D. (2022). Translanguaging as a decolonising approach: Students' perspectives towards integrating Indigenous epistemology in language teaching. *Applied Linguistics Review*, 1–22. https://doi.org/10.1515/applirev-2022-0127

Wigglesworth, G. (2020). Remote indigenous education and translanguaging. *TESOL in Context, 29*(1), 95–113.

Zavala, V. (2015). "It will emerge if they grow fond of it": Translanguaging and power in Quechua teaching. *Linguistics and Education, 32*, 16–26. https://doi.org/10.1016/j.linged.2015.01.009

CHAPTER 14

Translanguaging and Sustainable Development Goals

Abstract This chapter focuses on the integration of translanguaging practices in the context of achieving the Sustainable Development Goals (SDGs), particularly focusing on SDG 4 (Quality Education) and SDG 10 (Reduced Inequalities). It explores how translanguaging practices can enhance educational inclusivity through the integration of students' home languages into learning environments. Additionally, the chapter examines how translanguaging promotes social equity by empowering linguistic minorities and breaking down language barriers in various societal contexts. Practical examples illustrate how translanguaging can be implemented to foster inclusive education and reduce linguistic-based inequalities, thereby contributing to broader sustainable development efforts.

Keywords Sustainable Development Goals (SDGs) · Translanguaging · Educational inclusivity · Social equity · Linguistic minorities · SDG 4 · SDG 10 · Language barriers

The Sustainable Development Goals (SDGs) represent a global commitment to address pressing challenges and strive for a more equitable and sustainable world by 2030. Encompassing a broad spectrum of aspirations, from ending poverty and hunger to ensuring quality education and

© The Author(s), under exclusive license to Springer Nature Switzerland AG 2024
L. M. Pérez Fernández, *Translanguaging in Multicultural Societies*,
https://doi.org/10.1007/978-3-031-74145-6_14

reduced inequalities, the SDGs serve as a blueprint for collective action. Through facilitating cross-cultural understanding, enhancing inclusivity, and breaking down language barriers, translanguaging becomes instrumental in nurturing collaboration and collective efforts toward achieving some of these ambitious goals.

14.1   Multilingual Education and SDG 4 (Quality Education)

Sustainable Development Goal 4 (SDG 4) underscores the global commitment to ensure inclusive and equitable quality education for all by 2030 (United Nations General Assembly, 2015). With an emphasis on fostering lifelong learning opportunities, SDG 4 recognizes the transformative power of education in addressing socioeconomic disparities and building the foundation for sustainable development. In the pursuit of this goal, the intersection of multilingual education and SDG 4 becomes particularly significant, as it seeks to harness the benefits of linguistic diversity in educational settings. However, in many regions, the reliance on dominant global languages as the primary medium of instruction poses significant challenges, including limited access to education, higher dropout rates, and a disconnect between students' cultural backgrounds and educational experiences (Ojong & Addo, 2024). These challenges highlight the urgency of adopting multilingual approaches to education.

One of the primary contributions of translanguaging to SDG 4 lies in its ability to bridge language divides within the classroom. This implies incorporating students' home languages into the curriculum, instructional materials and classroom interactions, so educators create an inclusive and supportive environment where learners can engage more meaningfully with the content. For example, in multilingual classrooms, students educated solely in dominant languages often face challenges with comprehension and expression, which can lead to lower academic performance and reduced participation (Bamgbose, 2000). Mpofu (2021) demonstrates this in the context of African multilingual classrooms, where many students struggle with education delivered solely in colonial languages like English. By integrating home languages alongside dominant ones, translanguaging not only helps students better understand academic material but also addresses the inequities caused by monolingual policies, ensuring that linguistically diverse learners are not left behind.

Building on this idea, multilingual education and translanguaging practices contribute to breaking down barriers that might hinder access to quality education. Linguistically diverse students are often at risk of marginalization in monolingual educational systems, leading to disparities in academic achievement. Translanguaging mitigates these challenges by providing a more inclusive learning space where students can draw upon their full linguistic repertoire, enhancing their sense of belonging and empowerment. This approach also enables students to access information and educational resources in multiple languages, enhancing the accessibility and comprehensibility of learning. Furthermore, such practices support lifelong learning opportunities (Hashim, 2023), as students can utilize all their linguistic resources to engage with new content and ideas throughout their lives.

Beyond immediate educational outcomes, translanguaging promotes cultural competence and global citizenship, aligning with the broader objectives of SDG 4. As students engage in a multilingual learning environment where they develop language skills and cultivate a deeper understanding and appreciation for diverse cultures, they are prepared to actively participate in a globalized world. This participation contributes to the development of a more interconnected and harmonious society, supporting the goals of sustainable development.

To illustrate how translanguaging can be implemented to achieve SDG 4, here are two examples showcasing practical applications in different educational contexts.

Example 1: Bilingual peer tutoring programs

Bilingual peer tutoring programs are educational initiatives designed to leverage the linguistic strengths of students who are proficient in the school's primary language to support peers who speak a different home language. These programs support an inclusive learning environment by pairing students in a way that facilitates mutual learning and cultural exchange. Typically, such programs involve structured sessions where student pairs or small groups engage in collaborative learning activities, using both their home language and the school language to understand and master the curriculum. A way to put this into practice could be during scheduled study sessions, in which the pairs work together on their assignments and learning materials, using both languages to facilitate understanding and learning. For instance, in a science lesson on photosynthesis, the tutor can help the tutee read and understand a text in English, and then discuss and explain key concepts in Spanish. They can collaboratively create a summary in English, ensuring comprehension and reinforcing learning in both languages. Teachers can provide specific bilingual resources and guide the sessions, ensuring that both languages are actively used and respected. This approach promotes equity by overcoming linguistic barriers that could impede academic success.

Example 2: Multilingual reading circles

Reading circles, originally developed by Harvey Daniels in the 1990s, are small peer-led discussion groups designed to enhance students' higher-order thinking skills and promote lifelong reading habits (Daniels, 2002). These circles involve students choosing their own reading materials, forming temporary groups based on their book preferences, and engaging in structured discussions about the texts (Furr, 2004). To contribute to the achievement of SDG4, educators can implement multilingual reading circles that incorporate translanguaging principles. For instance, students might select reading materials in their preferred languages or in languages they are learning, forming small groups where they can discuss the texts using all available languages fluently known to them. Each group member takes on a specific role (e.g., discussion leader, summarizer, vocabulary wizard) that rotates after each reading cycle, encouraging comprehensive engagement with the text and promoting deeper understanding through collaborative learning. Students may summarize key points in their strongest language and use their other languages to clarify concepts while the teacher acts as a facilitator, guiding discussions to ensure meaningful exchanges and providing additional language support as needed. These circles create a supportive environment where linguistic diversity is used as a resource for deeper learning, thereby ensuring that all learners acquire the knowledge and skills needed to promote sustainable development.

In summary, the integration of translanguaging principles into Multilingual Education aligns with the aspirations of SDG 4. Through the acknowledgment and utilization of linguistic diversity, translanguaging promotes the creation of inclusive, equitable, and high-quality education opportunities, thereby advancing the global commitment to sustainable development.

14.2 Linguistic Diversity and SDG 10 (Reduced Inequalities)

Sustainable Development Goal 10 (SDG 10) addresses the imperative of reducing inequalities within and among countries (United Nations General Assembly, 2015). Focused on social, economic, and political dimensions, this goal seeks to ensure that the benefits of development are shared more equitably. The intersection of translanguaging and SDG 10 becomes particularly pertinent when considering linguistic diversity and its impact on societal inequalities.

Linguistic diversity, often associated with the coexistence of multiple languages within a society, is a dimension of diversity that cannot be overlooked in the pursuit of reduced inequalities (Liberali & Swanwick, 2020). Translanguaging, as a practice that embraces and values linguistic diversity, plays a crucial role in contributing to the objectives outlined in SDG 10. As Liberali & Swanwick (2020) illustrate in their study, translanguaging can act as a vehicle for decolonization, particularly in contexts where different social groups, such as the deaf and hearing communities, use multiple linguistic resources (including sign language and spoken language) to communicate and express shared emotional experiences. This intersection of languages and modalities fosters inclusive communication and challenges existing hierarchies within multilingual spaces.

A key contribution of translanguaging to SDG 10 lies in its potential to empower linguistic minorities, who often face discrimination and marginalization, thereby perpetuating broader inequalities. Translanguaging challenges this status quo by recognizing and validating the linguistic identities of minority groups. Liberali & Swanwick (2020) describe how translanguaging was used within the Digitmed Program to address broader social, political, and cultural injustices in educational settings. For example, during a literary soiree, deaf and hearing participants used gestures, facial expressions, and sign language alongside spoken word to collaboratively create meaning and address the emotional states conveyed in a poem. In such interactions, translanguaging becomes a tool for empowerment, allowing marginalized linguistic communities, such as deaf individuals, to assert their cultural identities and engage actively in societal discourse. As Liberali & Swanwick (2020) show, these interactions enable marginalized groups to transform their roles in society, from passive recipients of language to active creators of meaning.

Furthermore, reducing inequalities involves breaking down barriers that hinder access to essential services, information, and opportunities. Language barriers, in particular, can exacerbate disparities, limiting individuals' ability to fully participate in various aspects of life. Translanguaging promotes inclusivity by providing a means to overcome these language barriers. When public services, policies, and information are accessible in multiple languages, individuals from diverse linguistic backgrounds are better positioned to engage with and benefit from these resources, thus promoting a more equitable society.

Promoting inclusive policies and practices is another area where translanguaging contributes to SDG 10. Recognition and celebration of linguistic diversity go hand in hand with creating an environment that actively promotes inclusivity. Governments, institutions, and organizations that adopt policies supporting multilingualism contribute to reducing linguistic-based inequalities. Translanguaging, as both a pedagogical approach and a societal practice, nurtures environments where linguistic diversity is acknowledged and actively integrated into the structures and policies that shape society. Wei (2024) advocates for a mindset shift, arguing that the use of translanguaging in education should not simply be about allowing students to use their multiple languages in the classroom, but about understanding and valuing students' full linguistic identities. This involves recognizing how students' languages intersect with their racial and cultural identities, which can often be marginalized in traditional educational settings. Wei's framework of co-learning and transpositioning aligns with this approach, proposing that both teachers and students can undergo a shift in subjectivity, whereby teachers learn from students' diverse linguistic resources and students feel empowered to engage fully in the learning process.

Here are some examples of how translanguaging can be implemented to achieve SDG 10:

- Community-based language workshops:
  One strategy is to organize community-based language workshops that incorporate translanguaging to address linguistic diversity. These workshops can focus on practical skills, such as job interview preparation or accessing local services, and encourage participants to use multiple languages they are comfortable with, fostering better communication. While this approach can help reduce language barriers and promote social inclusion, it requires adequate resources,

trained facilitators, and community engagement to be effective in reducing linguistic inequalities.

- Educational support groups for migrant families:
  In educational settings, translanguaging can be instrumental in supporting migrant families who face language barriers. Educational support groups are established where bilingual facilitators and interpreters assist during parent-teacher meetings and school-related activities. These facilitators ensure that language does not hinder parents' participation in their children's education and empower families to engage meaningfully in educational decisions and activities. This approach fosters equal access to educational opportunities for children from migrant backgrounds, contributing directly to SDG 10's aim of reducing inequalities in education outcomes.

- Translanguaging in workplace training programs:
  The implementation of translanguaging practices in workplace training programs is a way to support employees from diverse linguistic backgrounds by promoting workplace equity and creating inclusive work environments where language differences do not hinder professional growth and success. Training sessions are conducted using bilingual materials and facilitated by bilingual trainers, ensuring that all employees can fully comprehend training content and actively participate in discussions and activities. This approach accommodates linguistic diversity in the workplace and enhances employee engagement, job satisfaction, and career development opportunities.

- Online language exchange platforms:
  Another way to support SDG 10 is through online language exchange platforms, designed to facilitate language exchange among people globally, employing translanguaging methods, therefore offering fair access to language learning resources and avenues for personal and professional development. Participants connect based on their language learning objectives and proficiency levels, engaging in conversations and activities where they switch between languages. These platforms facilitate cultural exchange, mutual learning, and collaboration across geographical boundaries. These exchanges promote global understanding and solidarity as they serve as a way to encourage individuals to value and learn from diverse linguistic and cultural contexts.

In conclusion, the incorporation of translanguaging principles aligns with the objectives of SDG 10 by addressing linguistic-based inequalities and encouraging inclusion. Translanguaging serves as a powerful tool to empower linguistic minorities, break down language barriers, and promote policies that actively reduce linguistic-based disparities, ultimately contributing to the broader goal of achieving a more equitable and just society.

REFERENCES

Bamgbose, A. (2000). *Language and exclusion: The consequences of language policies in Africa*. LIT Verlag.

Daniels, H. (2002). *Literature circles: Voice and choice in book clubs and reading groups*. Stenhouse Publishers.

Furr, M. (2004). Literature circles for the EFL classroom. In *Proceedings of the 2003 TESOL Arabia Conference*. TESOL Arabia.

Hashim, A. (2023). Literacy and lifelong learning in the twenty-first century: Development of multilingualism and multiliteracies in ASEAN. In W. O. Lee, P. Brown, A. L. Goodwin, & A. Green (Eds.), *International handbook on education development in Asia-Pacific* (pp. 1–15). Springer. https://doi.org/10.1007/978-981-16-2327-1_36-1

Liberali, F., & Swanwick, R. (2020). Translanguaging as a tool for decolonizing interactions in a space for confronting inequalities. *DELTA: Documentação de Estudos em Linguística Teórica e Aplicada, 36*(3). https://doi.org/10.1590/1678-460X2020360303

Mpofu, N. (2021). Possibilities of translanguaging pedagogy for sustainable education in Africa. In W. Leal Filho, R. Pretorius, & L. O. de Sousa (Eds.), *Sustainable development in Africa: Fostering sustainability in one of the world's most promising continents* (pp. 221–237). Springer

Ojong, A. S., & Addo, E. H. (2024). Advancing inclusivity, equity, and diversity in English language education: Empowering underrepresented students in Africa. *Journal of English Language Teaching and Applied Linguistics, 6*(2), 144–157. https://doi.org/10.32996/jeltal.2024.6.2.16

United Nations General Assembly. (2015). *Transforming our world: The 2030 Agenda for Sustainable Development* (A/RES/70/1). Retrieved November 27, 2024, from https://www.refworld.org/legal/resolution/unga/2015/en/111816

Wei, L. (2024). Transformative pedagogy for inclusion and social justice through translanguaging, co-learning, and transpositioning. *Language Teaching, 57*(2), 203–214. doi:10.1017/S0261444823000186

CHAPTER 15

Conclusion

Abstract This conclusion chapter provides a comprehensive summary of the book's exploration of translanguaging and its transformative impact across educational, communal, and professional domains. It encapsulates how translanguaging enhances inclusive education by valuing diverse linguistic backgrounds, fosters social integration within multicultural communities, and improves communication in various professional settings. Additionally, the chapter connects translanguaging practices to Sustainable Development Goals, highlighting their role in promoting linguistic diversity and reducing inequalities. The conclusion also outlines future directions for research, policy development, and the continued advocacy of translanguaging to build a more inclusive and sustainable society.

Keyword Translanguaging · Multilingual Education · Linguistic Diversity · Equity · Inclusion

Translanguaging, uncovered within these pages, emerges as a potent force with the capacity to reshape our educational, communal, and professional domains. It transcends being merely a linguistic phenomenon; driving transformative change in various contexts.

161
L. M. Pérez Fernández, *Translanguaging in Multicultural Societies*,
https://doi.org/10.1007/978-3-031-74145-6_15

In educational settings, the incorporation of translanguaging practices is poised to revolutionize language education. Traditionally, language education has often emphasized a monolingual approach, where students are expected to learn and communicate solely in one language. However, translanguaging challenges this approach recognizing and appreciating the diverse linguistic backgrounds of students. This involves creating inclusive learning environments that contribute to a richer exploration of language and culture, acknowledging and valuing the various languages that students bring to the classroom, and allowing them to use their full linguistic repertoire. In doing so, educators enable students to engage in meaningful language activities that go beyond strict language boundaries, thereby promoting a more inclusive atmosphere while deepening their understanding of both language and culture.

Despite recent efforts to incorporate a translanguaging approach in assessment, particularly in reading, speaking, and writing, there remains a notable absence of transmodality in their design. This gap underscores the need for a transformative shift in teacher perceptions and practices to bridge the divide between current limited efforts and a more comprehensive adoption of translanguaging in assessment. In both research and assessment practices, a significant gap exists, necessitating a thorough exploration of how a translanguaging approach can inform the development of transmodal assessment. Such an exploration is vital to ensuring that assessments in the classroom accurately and fairly evaluate students' knowledge and understanding.

Extending beyond classrooms, translanguaging makes its mark in multicultural communities. It becomes a key driver for social integration, community development, and the preservation of cultural heritage. Embracing translanguaging allows communities to value linguistic diversity, bridge cultural gaps, and promote social cohesion. In multicultural communities, where individuals may speak different languages and come from diverse cultural backgrounds, translanguaging becomes a powerful tool for enhancing social integration. Instead of viewing linguistic diversity as a barrier, this practice encourages individuals to use and appreciate multiple languages in their interactions, breaking down language barriers and promoting a sense of unity.

In professional spheres, translanguaging proves its worth as a valuable asset. Whether in business, healthcare, or legal contexts, the ability to adeptly use multiple languages enhances communication and understanding. This book has explored the legal and ethical dimensions of translanguaging in professional contexts, providing a thorough under-standing of its implications and responsibilities.

Peering into the future, translanguaging aligns with Sustainable Devel-opment Goals (SDGs), particularly in the areas of multilingual education and linguistic diversity. The integration of translanguaging practices supports SDG 4 (Quality Education) promoting inclusive and equitable education. Furthermore, it contributes to SDG 10 (Reduced Inequal-ities) recognizing and valuing the linguistic diversity within societies. Educational systems must embrace translanguaging pedagogies, equip-ping teachers to harness the multilingual capabilities of their students for enhanced educational outcomes. Additionally, policymakers and institu-tions bear the responsibility of formulating inclusive language policies that respect the vibrancy of linguistic diversity, ensuring equitable access and opportunities for all.

In the wake of this transformative potential, this book concludes with a call to action for future research and development in the field of translan-guaging. The evolving nature of this field demands a closer examination of transmodal assessment practices, moving beyond traditional literacy-dominant approaches. Furthermore, understanding teacher perceptions and practices in incorporating translanguaging into education is critical for effective implementation. The exploration of context-specific translan-guaging approaches tailored to different educational and cultural settings can significantly enhance their relevance and impact. Delving into the social and ethical dimensions of translanguaging in professional contexts can provide insights into issues related to equity, inclusion, and cultural sensitivity. Additionally, attention to policy implications and the formula-tion of inclusive language policies is crucial to ensure the celebration of linguistic diversity in educational institutions. Finally, longitudinal studies tracking the impact of translanguaging practices on language develop-ment, academic achievement, and social integration will contribute to evidence-based educational practices.

In summary, this book has sought to offer a thorough understanding of translanguaging, explore its implementation strategies, and advocate for its adoption to build a more inclusive and sustainable society. It highlights the potential for positive change in schools, communities, and profes-sional settings. The promotion of translanguaging practices can establish the groundwork for a more inclusive, interconnected, and sustainable future, where linguistic diversity is not just recognized but valued as a source of strength and enrichment.

REFERENCES

Abraham, S., Kedley, K., Fall, M., Krishnarmurthy, S., & Tulino, D. (2021). Creating a translanguaging space in a bilingual community-based writing program. *International Multilingual Research Journal*, *15*(3), 211–234. https://doi.org/10.1080/19313152.2021.1883791

Ahmed, F., & Abu Nayeem, M. (2023). Linguistic hybridity and cultural preservation: A qualitative exploration of cultural identity. *Journal of English Studies*, *1*(1), 85–99.

Achebe, C. (2006). *Things fall apart*. Penguin Classics.

Anchimbe, E. (2015). Code-switching: Between identity and exclusion. In G. Stell & K. Yakpo (Eds.), *Code-switching Between structural and sociolinguistic perspectives* (pp. 117–138). De Gruyter.

Angermeyer, P. S. (2005). Spelling bilingualism: Script choice in Russian American classified ads and signage. *Language in Society*, *34*(4), 493–531. https://doi.org/10.1017/S0047404505050190

Arredondo, M. M., Kovelman, I., Satterfield, T., Hu, X., Stojanov, L., & Beltz, A. M. (2022). Person-specific connectivity mapping uncovers differences of bilingual language experience on brain bases of attention in children. *Brain and Language*, *227*, 1–36. https://doi.org/10.1016/j.bandl.2022.105084

Asolati, G. (2022). *Shaping identity through bilingualism and translanguaging*. (PhD dissertation). https://thesis.unipd.it/retrieve/08e0a6c5-e833-4f8a-80e7-ba44d27319cd/Dissertation%20Giorgia%20Asolati.pdf

Baker, C. (2001, 2011). *Foundations of bilingual education and bilingualism*. Multilingual Matters.

Bakhtin, M. M. (1986). *Speech genres and other late essays*. University of Texas Press.

Basque Government. (2021). *VII Encuesta Sociolingüística 2021* [The Sociolinguistic Survey of the Basque Autonomous Community]. Department of Culture and Language Policy of the Basque Government. https://www.eustat.eus/elementos/ele0021500/vii-encuesta-sociolinguistica/inf0021552_c.pdf

Baumgardner, R. J. (2006). The appeal of English in Mexican commerce. *World Englishes, 25,* 251–266. https://doi.org/10.1111/j.0083-2919.2006.00463.x

Bautista-Thomas, C. M. (2015). Translanguaging and parental engagement. *Theory, Research and Action in Urban Education, 4*(1). https://traue.commons.gc.cuny.edu/volume-iv-issue-1-fall-2015/translanguaging-and-parental-engagement/

Bialystok, E., & Senman, L. (2004). Executive processes in appearance-reality tasks: The role of inhibition of attention and symbolic representation. *Child Development, 75,* 562–579. https://doi.org/10.1111/j.1467-8624.2004.00693.x

Bisai, S., & Singh, S. (2019). Bridging the divide: Collaborative learning and translanguaging in multilingual classrooms. *A Journal of Teaching English Language and Literature, 39,* 46–57.

Blommaert, J. (2012). Supervernaculars and their dialects. *Dutch Journal of Applied Linguistics, 1*(1), 1–14. https://doi.org/10.1075/dujal.1.1.03blo

Blommaert, J. (2014). From mobility to complexity in sociolinguistic theory and method. In N. Coupland (Ed.), *Sociolinguistics: Theoretical debates* (pp. 242–260). Cambridge University Press.

Blommaert, J., & Rampton, B. (2011). *Language and Superdiversity. Diversities, 13*(2), 1–21.

Bonacina-Pugh, F., Da Costa Cabral, I., & Huang, J. (2021). Translanguaging in education. *Language Teaching: Surveys and Studies, 54*(4), 439–471. https://doi.org/10.1017/S0261444821000173

Brass, P. R. (2005). *Language, religion, and politics in North India.* iUniverse.

Brooks, E. (2022). Translanguaging health. *Applied Linguistics, 43*(3), 517–537. https://doi.org/10.1093/applin/amab054

Canagarajah, S. (2007). The ecology of global English. *International Multidisciplinary Research Journal, 1*(2), 89–100. https://doi.org/10.1080/15257770701495299

Canagarajah, S. (2011a). Translanguaging in the classroom: Emerging issues for research and pedagogy. *Applied Linguistics Review, 2,* 1–28. https://doi.org/10.1515/9783110239331.1

Canagarajah, S. (2011b). Codemeshing in academic writing: Identifying teachable strategies of translanguaging. *The Modern Language Journal, 95*(3), 401–417. https://doi.org/10.1111/j.1540-4781.2011.01207.x

Canals, L. (2023). Translanguaging practices and metalinguistic reflection during negotiation of meaning in tandem virtual exchanges. *Bellaterra Journal of Teaching & Learning Language & Literature, 16*(3), 1–19.

Carter, H., & Bradford, M. (2019). Opening the window to a world wider than our little classroom. The importance of culturally relevant pedagogy. *EViE: Emerging Voices in Education, 1*(1), 18–32.

Cenoz, J., & Gorter, D. (2015). Towards a holistic approach in the study of multilingual education. In J. Cenoz & D. Gorter (Eds.), *Multilingual education: Between language learning and translanguaging* (pp. 1–15). Cambridge University Press.

Cenoz, J., & Gorter, D. (2017). Minority languages and sustainable translanguaging: Threat or opportunity? *Journal of Multilingual and Multicultural Development, 38*, 901–912. https://doi.org/10.1080/01434632.2017.128 4855

Cenoz, J., & Gorter, D. (2022). Pedagogical translanguaging and its application to language classes. *RELC Journal, 53*(2), 342–354. https://doi.org/ 10.1177/00336882221082751

Cioè-Peña, M., & Snell, T. (2015). Translanguaging for social justice. *Theory, Research, and Action in Urban Education, IV*(1). https://traue.commons.gc.cuny.edu/volume-iv-issue-1-fall-2015/translanguaging-for-social-justice/

Cook V. (1991). The poverty-of-the-stimulus argument and multi-competence. *Second Language Research, 7*(2), 103–117. https://www.jstor.org/stable/ 43104425

Cook, V. (2016). Premises of multi-competence. In V. Cook & W. Li (Eds.), *The Cambridge handbook of linguistic multicompetence* (pp. 1–25). Cambridge University Press.

Council of Europe. (2011). *The European Language Portfolio.* www.coe.int/en/ web/portfolio

Council of Europe. (2018). *Common European framework of reference for languages: Learning, teaching, assessment. Companion Volume with New Descriptors.* Council of Europe Publishing. https://rm.coe.int/cefr-compan ion-volume-with-new-descriptors-2018/1680787989

Creese, A., & Blackledge, A. (2010). Translanguaging in the bilingual classroom: A pedagogy for learning and teaching? *The Modern Language Journal, 94*(1), 103–115. https://doi.org/10.1111/j.1540-4781.2009.00986.x

Creese, A., & Blackledge, A. (2015). Translanguaging and identity in educational settings. *Annual Review of Applied Linguistics, 35*, 20–35. https://doi.org/ 10.1017/S0267190514000233

Creese, A., & Blackledge, A. (2019). Translanguaging and Public service encounters: Language learning in the library. *The Modern Language Journal, 103*(4), 800–814. https://doi.org/10.1111/modl.12601

Crisostomo, C. J. (2020). Sumerian and Akkadian language contact. In R. Hasselbach-Andee (Ed.), *A companion to ancient near eastern languages* (pp. 401–420). Wiley-Blackwell.

Cummins, J. (2007). Rethinking monolingual instructional strategies in multilingual classrooms. *Canadian Journal of Applied Linguistics, 10,* 221–240.

Cummins, J. (2008). Teaching for transfer: Challenging the two solitudes assumptions in bilingual education. In N. H. Hornberger (Ed.), *Encyclopedia of language and education* (pp. 1528–1538). Springer.

Daniels, H. (2002). *Literature circles: Voice and choice in book clubs and reading groups.* Stenhouse Publishers.

De Bot, K., Lowie, W., & Verspoor, M. (2007). A dynamic systems theory approach to second language acquisition. *Bilingualism: Language and Cognition, 10*(1), 7–21. https://doi.org/10.1017/S1366728906002732

DeFalco, A. K. (2023). Translanguaging as a tool for equity in classroom assessment. *MinneTESOL Journal, 39*(1), 1–6.

Del Corro, A. (2020). The Pinoy version: A revelation. *The Bible Translator, 71*(1), 18–37.

Demir, M. (2017). The translation activities of Andalus period. *European Journal of Literature, Language and Linguistic Studies, 1*(1), 13–23. https://doi.org/10.5281/zenodo.837843

Dijkstra, T., & van Heuven, W. J. B. (2002). The architecture of the bilingual visual word recognition system: From identification to decision. *Bilingualism: Language and Cognition, 5*(3), 175–197.

Duarte, J. (2018). Translanguaging in the context of mainstream multilingual education. *International Journal of Multilingualism, 17*(2), 232–247. https://doi.org/10.1080/14790718.2018.1512607

Duarte, J., & Kirsch, C. (2020). Introduction: Multilingual approaches for teaching and learning. In C. Kirsch & J. Duarte (Eds.), *Multilingual approaches for teaching and learning: from acknowledging to capitalising on multilingualism in European mainstream education* (pp. 17–27). Routledge. https://doi.org/10.4324/9780429059674-1

Dumrukcic, N. (2020). Translanguaging in social media. Output for FLT didactics. *HeiEducation Journal, 5,* 109–137. https://doi.org/10.17885/heiup.heied.2020.5

Dumrukcic, N. (2022). *Translanguaging and the bilingual brain.* De Gruyter.

Fang, F., Zhang, L. J., & Sah, P. K. (2022). Translanguaging in language teaching and learning: Current practices and future directions. *RELC Journal, 53*(2), 305–312. https://doi.org/10.1177/00336882221114478

Ferguson, C. A. (1959). Diglossia. *Word, 15*(2), 325–340. https://doi.org/10.1080/00437956.1959.11659702

Fishman, J. A. (1991). *Reversing language shift: Theoretical and empirical foundations of assistance to threatened languages.* Multilingual Matters.

Fithri, S. (2019). An overview of indigenous language programs in Australian and New Zealand. *Advances in Social Science, Education and Humanities Research*, volume 254, Eleventh Conference on Applied Linguistics (CONAPLIN 2018), 250–254.

Flavell, J. H. (1979). Metacognition and cognitive monitoring: A new area of cognitive–developmental inquiry. *American Psychologist, 34*(10), 906–911. https://doi.org/10.1037/0003-066X.34.10.906

Flores, N., & Lewis, M. (2016). From truncated to sociopolitical emergence: A critique of super-diversity in sociolinguistics. *International Journal of the Sociology of Language, 241*, 97–124. https://doi.org/10.1515/ijsl-2016-0024

Fox, J. J., & Babo Soares, D. (2003). *Out of the Ashes: Destruction and reconstruction of East Timor*. ANU Press. https://doi.org/10.26530/oapen_459402

Furr, M. (2004). Literature circles for the EFL classroom. In *Proceedings of the 2003 TESOL Arabia Conference*. TESOL Arabia.

Futro, D. (2023). *Translanguaging art: multilingual practices of contemporary artists and their implications for language pedagogy* (PhD thesis). University of Glasgow.

Galante, A. (2020). Translanguaging for vocabulary improvement: A mixed methods study with international students in a Canadian EAP program. In T. Zhongfeng, L. Aghai, P. Sayer, & J. L. Schissel (Eds.), *Envisioning TESOL through a translanguaging lens* (pp. 93–328). Springer.https://doi.org/10.1007/978-3-030-47031-9_14

Gallego, M. A. (2003). The languages of Medieval Iberia and their religious dimension. *Medieval Encounters, 9*(1), 107–139.

García, O. (2009a). *Bilingual education in the 21st century: A global perspective*. Wiley-Blackwell.

García, O. (2009b). Education, multilingualism and translanguaging in the 21st century. In T. Skutnabb-Kangas, R. Phillipson, A. Mohanty, & M. Panda (Ed.), *Social justice through multilingual education* (pp. 140–158). Multilingual Matters. https://doi.org/10.21832/9781847691910-011

García, O., & Leiva, C. (2014). Theorizing and enacting translanguaging for social justice. In A. Blackledge & A. Creese (Eds.), *Heteroglossia as practice and pedagogy* (pp. 199–216). Springer. https://doi.org/10.1007/978-94-007-7856-6_11

García, O., & Otheguy, R. (2019). Plurilingualism and translanguaging: Commonalities and divergences. *International Journal of Bilingual Education and Bilingualism, 23*(1), 17–35. https://doi.org/10.1080/13670050.2019.1598932

García, O., & Li, W. (2014). *Translanguaging: Language, bilingualism and education*. Palgrave Macmillan.

Gilmartin, M. (2004). Language, education and the New South Africa. *Tijdschrift Voor Economische En Sociale Geografie, 95*(4), 405–418.

Gómez, M. M. (2000). La lengua "aljamiada" y su literatura: una variante islámica del español. *Castilla: Estudios de literatura, 25,* 71–83

Goos, M., Galbraith, P., & Renshaw, P. (2002). Socially mediated metacognition: Creating collaborative zones of proximal development in small group problem solving. *Educational Studies in Mathematics, 49,* 193–223. https://doi.org/10.1023/A:1016209010120

Gorter, D., & Cenoz, J. (2015). The linguistic landscapes inside multilingual schools. In B. Spolsky, M. Tannenbaum, & O. Inbar (Eds.), *Challenges for language education and policy: Making space for people* (pp. 151–169). Routledge Publishers.

Government of Canada. (2024). *Indigenous Languages and Cultures Program.* https://www.canada.ca/en/canadian-heritage/services/funding/aboriginal-peoples.html

Gray, E. G., & Fiering, N. (2000). *The language encounter in the Americas, 1492–1800.* Berghahn Books.

Groeneboer, K. (1998). *Gateway to the West. The Dutch language in Colonial Indonesia 1600–1950. A history of language policy.* Amsterdam University Press.

Grosjean, F. (1982). *Life with two languages.* Harvard University Press.

Grosjean, F. (1985). The bilingual as a competent but specific speaker–hearer. *Journal of Multilingual and Multicultural Development, 6*(6), 467–477. https://doi.org/10.1080/01434632.1985.9994221

Grosjean, F. (1989). Neurolinguists, beware! The bilingual is not two monolinguals in one person. *Brain and Language, 36*(1), 3–15. https://doi.org/10.1016/0093-934x(89)90048-5

Ha, T. T. T., Phan, T. T. N., & Anh, T. H. (2021). The importance of translanguaging in improving fluency in speaking ability of Non-English major sophomores. *Advances in Social Science, Education and Humanities Research, 621,* 338–344. https://doi.org/10.2991/assehr.k.211224.032

Hajek, J. (2002). *Language maintenance and survival in East Timor: All change now?* Routledge.

Han, J. (2023). *English medium instruction as a local practice. Language, culture and pedagogy.* Springer.

Han, X., Li, W., & Filippi, R. (2022). The effects of habitual code-switching in bilingual language production on cognitive control. *Bilingualism: Language and Cognition, 25*(5), 869–889. https://doi.org/10.1017/S1366728922000244

Harvey, S. P., & Rivett, S. (2017). Colonial-Indigenous language encounters in North America and the intellectual history of the Atlantic World. *Early*

American Studies: An Interdisciplinary Journal, *15*(3), 442–473. https://doi.org/10.1353/eam.2017.0017

Hatcher, T., & Son, S. (2022). Translanguaging: Leveraging multilingualism for scripture engagement. *The Bible Translator*, *73*(1), 120–140. https://doi.org/10.1177/20516770211062143

Haugen, E. (1972). The ecology of language. In A. S. Dil (Ed.), *The ecology of language: Essays by Einar Haugen*. Stanford University Press.

Hiroyuki, M. (2002). *Colonial language policies and their effects*. World Congress on Language Policies. Barcelona 16–20 April. https://www.linguapax.org/wp-content/uploads/2015/07/CMPL2002_T1_MHiroyuki.pdf

Hosington, B. M. (2015). Introduction: Translation and print culture in early modern Europe. *Renaissance Studies*, *29*(1), 5–18. http://www.jstor.org/stable/26631746

Hull, G. (2001). *Standard Tetum-English dictionary*. Allen & Unwin in association with the University of Western Sydney.

Iliescu, C. (2017). Arguments for a translanguaging approach to the case of Romanian Diaspora in Spain. *Philologica Jassyensia*, *2*(26), 281–293.

Ishii, D., & Takagaki, T. (2021). Translanguaging in healthcare websites: Implications for language policy and social cohesion. *Language and Linguistics in Oceania*, *13*, 86–101.

Jonsson, C., & Blasjö, M. (2020). Translanguaging and multimodality in workplace texts and writing. *International Journal of Multilingualism*, *17*(3), 361–381. https://doi.org/10.1080/14790718.2020.1766051

Katz, S. J., & Byrne, S. (2019). Cognitive bridging: Using strategic communication to connect abstract goals with the means to achieve them. *Health Communication*, *34*(4), 484–499. https://doi.org/10.1080/10410236.2018.1428848

Kim, D., Lim, J. H., & An, J. (2022). The quality and effectiveness of Social-Emotional Learning (SEL) intervention studies in Korea: A meta-analysis. *PLoS ONE*, *17*(6), 1–18. https://doi.org/10.1371/journal.pone.0269996

Kleeman, C. (2021). Pedagogical Translanguaging to create sustainable minority language practices in kindergarten. *Sustainability*, *13*(7), 1–19. https://doi.org/10.3390/su13073613

Kovelman, I., Baker, S. A., & Petitto, L. A. (2008). Bilingual and monolingual brains compared: A functional magnetic resonance imaging investigation of syntactic processing and a possible "neural signature" of bilingualism. *Journal of Cognitive Neuroscience*, *20*(1), 153–169. https://doi.org/10.1162/jocn.2008.20011

Krashen, S. D. (1982). *Principles and practice in second language acquisition*. Pergamon Press Inc.

Labov, William. (1972). *Sociolinguistic patterns*. University of Pennsylvania Press.

Lambert, J. (2012). In place of foreword. In C. Iliescu Gheorghiu (Cord.), *Traducción y (a)culturación en la era global* (pp. 9–10). Agua Clara.

Lankiewicz, H. A. (2021). Linguistic hybridity and learner identity: translingual practice among plurilinguals in the educational setting. *Czasopismo Polskiego Towarzystwa Neofilologicznego*, 56(1), 55–70. https://doi.org/10.14746/n.2021.56.1.5

Larsen-Freeman, D. (2020). Chaos/complexity theory for second language acquisition/development. In C. A. Chapellep (Ed.), *The encyclopedia of applied linguistics* (pp. 1–8). Wiley-Blackwell. https://doi.org/10.1002/978 1405198431.wbeal0125

Leonet, O., Cenoz, J., & Gorter, D. (2017). Challenging minority language isolation: Translanguaging in a trilingual school in the Basque country. *Journal of Language, Identity & Education*, 16(4), 216–227. https://doi.org/10.1080/15348458.2017.1328281

Lewis, G., Jones, B., & Baker, C. (2012a). Translanguaging: Origins and development from school to street and beyond. *Education Research and Evaluation*, 18(7), 641–654. https://doi.org/10.1080/13803611.2012.718488

Lewis, G., Jones, B., & Baker, C. (2012b). Translanguaging: Developing its conceptualisation and contextualisation. *Education Research and Evaluation*, 18(7), 655–670. https://doi.org/10.1080/13803611.2012.718490

Li, W. (2000). Dimensions of bilingualism. In W. Li (Ed.), *The bilingualism reader* (pp. 3–25). Routledge.

Li, W. (2018). Translanguaging as a practical theory of language. *Applied Linguistics*, 1, 9–30. https://doi.org/10.1093/applin/amx039

Li, W. (2024). Transformative pedagogy for inclusion and social justice through translanguaging, co-learning, and transpositioning. *Language Teaching*, 57(2), 203–214. https://doi.org/10.1017/S0261444823000186

Li, W., & García, O. (2022). Not a first language but one repertoire: Translanguaging as a decolonizing project. *RELC Journal*, 53(2), 313–324. https://doi.org/10.1177/00336882221092841

Liddicoat, A. J., & Bryant, P. (2001). Language planning and language revival: A current issue in language planning. *Current Issues in Language Planning*, 2(2–3), 137–140. https://doi.org/10.1080/14664200108668022

Lopez, A. A., Turkan, S., & Guzman-Orth, G. (2017). Conceptualizing the use of translanguaging in initial content assessments for newly arrived emergent bilingual students. *ETS Research Report Series*, 1, 1–12. https://doi.org/10.1002/ets2.12140

Lumban Batu, P., & Sukamto, K. (2020). Translanguaging practices in Indonesian pop songs. *ELS Journal on Interdisciplinary Studies in Humanities*, 3(2), 308–316. https://doi.org/10.34050/els-jish.v3i2.9706

Luo, X. (2020). Translation and diaspora literature. *Asia Pacific Translation and Intercultural Studies, 7*(1), 1–2. https://doi.org/10.1080/23306343.2020. 1748796

Madianou, M. (2014). Polymedia communication and Mediatized migration. In K. Lundby (Ed.), *Mediatization of communication* (pp. 323–348). De Gruyter.

Maia, M., Nascimento, M., & Whan, C. (2018). The Maori language nest program: Voices of language and culture revitalization in Aotearoa, New Zealand. *Ecolingüística: Revista Brasileira de Ecologia e Linguagem, 4*(1), 108–127.

Makalela, L. (2015). Moving out of linguistic boxes: The effects of translanguaging strategies for multilingual classrooms. *Language and Education, 29*(3), 200–2017. https://doi.org/10.1080/09500782.2014.994524

Makalela, L. (2016). Ubuntu translanguaging: An alternative framework for complex multilingual encounters. *Southern African Linguistics and Applied Language Studies, 34*(3), 187–196. https://doi.org/10.2989/16073614. 2016.1250350

Makalela, L., & Aparecido da Silva, K. (2023). Ubuntu translanguaging: a decolonial model for the Global South multilingualism. *Revista Linguagem & Ensino, 26*(1), 84–97. https://doi.org/10.15210/rle.v26i1.6804

Makoni, S., & Pennycook, A. (2007). *Disinventing and reconstituting languages.* Multilingual Matters.

Mantel, S., & Kellaris, J. (2023). Bilingual signs: How language influences shoppers. *Interdisciplinary Journal of Signage and Wayfinding, 7*(1), 5–20.

Margana., & Rasman. (2021). Translanguaging and Minoritized language maintenance: Lessons from Indonesia. *3L: Language, Linguistics, Literature. The Southeast Asian Journal of English Language Studies, 27*(2), 1–15. https://doi.org/10.17576/3L-2021-2702-01

Marian, V., & Spivey, M. (2003). Bilingual and monolingual processing of competing lexical items. *Applied Psycholinguistics, 24*(2), 173–193. https://doi.org/10.1017/S0142716403000092

Mateos-Aparicio, P., & Rodríguez-Moreno, A. (2019). The impact of studying brain plasticity. *Frontiers in Cellular Neuroscience, 13*, 1–5. https://doi.org/10.3389/fncel.2019.00066

McCaffrey, K. T., & Taha, M. C. (2019). Rethinking the digital divide: Smartphones as translanguaging tools among Middle Eastern Refugees in New Jersey. *Annals of Anthropological Practice, 43*(2), 26–38. https://doi.org/10.1111/napa.12126

Meletiadou, E. (2022). The utilisation of peer-assisted learning/mentoring and translanguaging in higher education. *IAFOR Journal of Education: Language Learning in Education, 10*(1), 135–154.

Mora, R. A., Tian, Z., & Harman, R. (2022). Translanguaging and multi-modality as flow, agency, and a new sense of advocacy in and from the Global South. *Pedagogies: An International Journal, 17*(4), 271–281. https://doi.org/10.1080/1554480X.2022.2143089

Namatama, K. B., & Jimaima, H. (2020). Translanguaging as commodified semiotic resource among traders and customers of Soweto Market in Lusaka Zambia. *Multidisciplinary Journal of Language and Social Sciences Education, 3*(2), 229–249.

Nnenna, E., & I., A., O., Umeh, E., Chikaodi, A. (2022). Code switching and code mixing in teaching and learning of English as a second language: Building on knowledge. *English Language Teaching, 15*(9), 106–106. https://doi.org/10.5539/elt.v15n9p106

Ng, B. C., & Cavallaro, F. (2021). Where have all my languages gone? Aging and the changing multilingual linguistic ecology. In R. Blackwood & U. Røyneland (Eds.), *Trajectories of language: policies, spaces and interactions. Volume I: Multilingualism Across the Lifespan*, (pp. 147–168). Routledge. https://doi.org/10.4324/9781003125815-7

Ng, L. L., & Lee, S. L. (2019). Translanguaging practices and identity construction of multilingual Malaysian university graduates in digital media. *English Teaching & Learning, 43*, 105–123. https://doi.org/10.1007/s42321-019-00021-6

Nikeghbal, N., & Yüncü, H. R. (2022). Reflection of Turkish-Persian linguistic interaction on Turkish Cuisine. *Journal of Tourism and Gastronomy Studies, 10*(3), 1908–1923. https://doi.org/10.21325/jotags.2022.1073

Ocampo, D. (2023). Translanguaging and reading comprehension of Filipino ESL intermediate learners. *Journal of Natural Language and Linguistics, 1*(1), 13–21. https://doi.org/10.54536/jnll.v1i1.1510

Odlin, T. (1989). *Language transfer. Cross-linguistic influence in language learning*. Cambridge University Press.

Oliver, R., Wigglesworth, G., Angelo, D., & Steele, C. (2021). Translating translanguaging into our classrooms: Possibilities and challenges. *Language Teaching Research, 25*(1), 134–150. https://doi.org/10.1177/1362168820938822

Pennycook, A. (2010). *Language as a local practice*. Routledge.

Piller, I. (2015). Language ideologies. In K. Tracy, C. Ilie, & T. Sandel (Eds.), *The International encyclopedia of language and social interaction* (Vol. 2, pp. 917–927). (The Wiley Blackwell-ICA international encyclopedias of communication). Wiley-Blackwell.

Poplack, S. (1980). Sometimes I'll start a sentence in Spanish y termino en español: Toward a typology of code-switching. *Linguistics, 18*, 581–618. https://doi.org/10.1515/ling.1980.18.7-8.581

Portolés, L., & Martí, O. (2017). Translanguaging as a teaching resource in early language learning of English as an additional language (EAL). *Bellaterra Journal of Teaching & Learning Language & Literature, 10*(1), 61–77. https://doi.org/10.5565/rev/jtl3.698

Prnjat, D. (2019). Culture and communication: A look at the Hellenistic Mediterranean. In D. K. Vukcevic & P. Rudan (Eds.), *MASA-EMAN Symposium. culture, technology and humanism.* Montenegrin Academy of Sciences and Arts.

Quentin Dixon, L. (2005). Bilingual education policy in Singapore: An analysis of its sociohistorical roots and current academic outcomes. *International Journal of Bilingual Education and Bilingualism, 8*(1), 25–47. https://doi.org/10.1080/jBEB.v8.i1.pg25

Rabbidge, M. (2019). The effects of translanguaging on participation in EFL classrooms. *The Journal of Asia TEFL, 16*(4), 1305–1322. https://doi.org/10.18823/asiatefl.2019.16.4.15.1305

Rajendram, S. (2021). The cognitive-conceptual, planning-organizational, affective-social and linguistic-discursive affordances of translanguaging. *Applied Linguistics Review, 14*(5), 1185–1218. https://doi.org/10.1515/applirev-2020-0075

Ray, A., Sarangi, P., Purohit, B., & Dash, S. R. (2023). Three language formula in national education policy, 2020 of India: From the Stakeholder's perspectives. *Journal of Higher Education Theory and Practice, 23*(13), 136–154. https://doi.org/10.33423/jhetp.v23i13.6369

Richardson, B. (2023). Multilingual Printing. In A. Petrocchi & J. Brown (Eds.), *Languages and cross-cultural exchanges in renaissance Italy* (pp. 35–64). Brepols Publishers.

Robillos R. J. (2023). Exploring Translanguaging during metacognitive strategy use on L2 listening and writing skills. *Journal of Language and Education, 9*(3), 110–128. https://doi.org/10.17323/jle.2023.14329

Roy, A. (1997). *The god of small things.* Thorndike.

Rowe, M. L., Silverman, R. D., & Mullan, B. E. (2013). The role of pictures and gestures as nonverbal aids in preschoolers' word learning in a novel language. *Contemporary Educational Psychology, 38*(2), 109–117. https://doi.org/10.1016/j.cedpsych.2012.12.001

Safran, W. (1991). Diasporas in modern societies: Myths of homeland and return. *Diaspora: A Journal of Transnational Studies, 1*(1), 83–99.

Salverda, R. (2014). Between Dutch and Indonesian: Colonial Dutch in time and space. In F. Hinskens & J. Taeldeman (Ed.), *Volume 3 Dutch* (pp. 800–821). De Gruyter Mouton. https://doi.org/10.1515/9783110261332.800

Sánchez, M. T., García, O., & Solorza, C. (2018). Reframing language allocation policy in dual language bilingual education. *Bilingual Research Journal, 41*(1), 37–51. https://doi.org/10.1080/15235882.2017.1405098

Sanchez-Stockhammer, C. (2012). Hybridization in language. In P. W. Stock-hammer (Ed.), *Conceptualizing cultural hybridization: A transdisciplinary approach* (pp. 133–157). Springer. https://doi.org/10.1007/978-3-642-218 46-0_9

Sato, R. (2023). Japanese EFL Speakers' willingness to communicate in L2 conversations: The Effects of code-switching and translanguaging. *The Electronic Journal for English as a Second Language, 27*(3), 1–22. https://doi.org/10.55593/ej.27107a5

Schaefer, C. (2010). Multilingualism and language contact in urban centres along the Silk Road during the first millennium AD. In P. J. J. Sinclair, G. Nordquist, F. Herschend, & C. Isendahl (Eds.), *The urban mind: Cultural and Environmental dynamics* (pp. 441–455). Uppsala University.

Schiffman, H. (1996). *Linguistic culture and language policy*. Routledge.

Schissel, J., De Korne, H., & López-Gopar, M. (2021). Grappling with translanguaging for teaching and assessment in culturally and linguistically diverse contexts: Teacher perspectives from Oaxaca, Mexico. *International Journal of Bilingual Education and Bilingualism, 24*(3), 340–356. https://doi.org/10. 1080/13670050.2018.1463965

Selinker, L. (1972). Interlanguage. *International Review of Applied Linguistics, 10*, 209–231.

Sohn, B., dos Santos, P., & Lin, A. (2022). Translanguaging as a theory of language for a critical integration of content and language in multilingual educational settings. *RELC Journal, 53*(2), 355–370. https://doi.org/10. 1177/00336882221114480

Sorensen, A. (1967). Multilingualism in the Northwest Amazon. *American Anthropologist, 69*, 670–684.

Spilioti, T. (2019). From transliteration to trans-scripting: Creativity and multilingual writing on the internet. *Discourse, Context & Media, 29*, 1–10. https://doi.org/10.1016/j.dcm.2019.03.001

Steele, C., Dovchin, S., & Oliver, R. (2022). 'Stop measuring black kids with a white stick': Translanguaging for classroom assessment. *RELC Journal, 53*(2), 400–415. https://doi.org/10.1177/00336882221086307

Stenzel, K., & Khoo, V. (2016). Linguistic hybridity: A case study in the Kotiria community. *Critical Multilingualism Studies, 4*(2), 75–110.

Stille, S. V. V., Bethke, R., Bradley-Brown, J., Giberson, J., & Hall, G. (2016). Broadening educational practice to include translanguaging: An outcome of educator inquiry into multilingual students' learning needs. *Canadian Modern Language Review, 72*(4), 480–503. https://doi.org/10.3138/cmlr.3432

Stroud, C. (2007). 21. Multilingualism in ex-colonial countries. In P. Auer & L. Li (Ed.), *Handbook of multilingualism and multilingual communication* (pp. 509–538). De Gruyter Mouton. https://doi.org/10.1515/978311019 8553.4.509

Sun, M. S. (2013). Code-switching and translanguaging: Potential functions in multilingual classrooms. *Studies in Applied Linguistics & TESOL, 13*(2), 50–52. https://doi.org/10.7916/salt.v13i2.1332

Sun, W., Qiu, Y., & Zheng, Y. (2021). Translanguaging practices in local employees' negotiation to create linguistic space in a multilingual workplace. *Círculo De Lingüística Aplicada a La Comunicación, 86*, 31–42. https://doi.org/10.5209/clac.75493

Sun, P. P., & Zhang, L. J. (2022). Effects of translanguaging in online peer feedback on Chinese university English-as-a-foreign-language students' writing performance. *RELC Journal, 53*(2), 325–341. https://doi.org/10.1177/00336882221089051

Tajfel, H., & Turner, J. C. (1979). An integrative theory of inter-group conflict. In W. G. Austin & S. Worchel (Eds.), *The social psychology of inter-group relations* (pp. 33–47). Brooks/Cole.

Tham, I., Chau, M. H., & Thang, S. M. (2019). Bilinguals' processing of lexical cues in L1 and L2: An eye-tracking study. *Computer Assisted Language Learning, 33*(7), 665–687. https://doi.org/10.1080/09588221.2019.1588329

Tsokalidou, R., & Skourtou, E. (2020). Translanguaging as a culturally sustaining pedagogical approach: Bi/Multilingual educators' perspectives. In J. A. Panagiotopoulou, L. Rosen, & J. Strzykala (Eds.), *Inclusion, education and translanguaging* (pp. 219–235). Springer. https://doi.org/10.1007/978-3-658-28128-1_1

Van den Berghe, R. (2022). Social robots in a translanguaging pedagogy: A review to identify opportunities for robot-assisted (language) learning. *Frontiers in Robotics and AI, 9*, 1–8. https://doi.org/10.3389/frobt.2022.958624

Vygotsky, L. S. (1978). *Mind in society: The development of higher psychological processes*. Harvard University Press.

Walker, U. (2018). Translanguaging: Affordances for collaborative language learning. *New Zealand Studies in Applied Linguistics, 24*(1), 1–18.

Wang, D. (2022). Translanguaging as a decolonising approach: Students' perspectives towards integrating Indigenous epistemology in language teaching. *Applied Linguistics Review*, 1–22. https://doi.org/10.1515/applirev-2022-0127

Wang, R. (2023). An analysis of the influence of French colonization on the Vietnamese education system. *Interdisciplinary Humanities and Communication Studies, 1*(1), 1–14. https://doi.org/10.61173/aj42qn74

Wang, W., & Curdt-Christiansen, X. L. (2019). Translanguaging in a Chinese-English bilingual education programme: A university-classroom ethnography. *International Journal of Bilingual Education and Bilingualism, 22*(3), 322–337. https://doi.org/10.1080/13670050.2018.1526254

Wang, Y., & Phillion, J. (2009). Minority language policy and practice in China: The need for multicultural education. *International Journal of Multicultural Education*, *11*(1), 1–14. https://doi.org/10.18251/ijme.v11i1.138

Wigglesworth, G. (2020). Remote indigenous education and translanguaging. *TESOL in Context*, *29*(1), 95–113.

Williams, C. (1996). Secondary education: Teaching in the bilingual situation. In C. Williams, G. Lewis, & C. Baker (Eds.), *The language policy: Taking stock* (pp. 39–78). CAI Language Studies Centre.

Xu, W. (2024). Translanguaging practices and language ideologies in adult migrants' Chinese learning classrooms and beyond. *Journal of Multilingual and Multicultural Development*, 1–17. https://doi.org/10.1080/01434632.2024.2365321

Zavala, V. (2015). It will emerge if they grow fond of it: Translanguaging and power in Quechua teaching. *Linguistics and Education*, *32*, 16–26. https://doi.org/10.1016/j.linged.2015.01.009

INDEX

The manufacturer's authorised representative in the EU is Springer
Nature Customer Service Centre GmbH, Europaplatz 3, 69115 Heidelberg,
Germany. If you have any concerns regarding our products, please
contact ProductSafety@springernature.com

Printed and bound by CPI Group (UK) Ltd, Croydon, CR0 4YY
24/04/2026
02096368-0003